Dymphna Baird is originally from Crossgar, Northern Ireland. She left in the '70s to train as a primary school teacher in Newcastle upon Tyne.

Throughout her teaching career, she has taught in South Ockendon; Waltham Cross; Hertfordshire; Enfield; and an elementary school in Prince Rupert, British Columbia. She presently lives in Southgate, North London. She is married and has three sons, a twenty-five-year-old and twenty-four-year-old twins. After the birth of her children, she had a career break. When she returned to teaching, she became a qualified mentor and completed a degree in Psychology.

For my husband, Matthew; and sons, Will, Thomas and James, who have taught me the meaning of love.

Dymphna Baird

PILGRIMAGE TO THE HEART OF GOD

AUSTIN MACAULEY PUBLISHERS™

LONDON • CAMBRIDGE • NEW YORK • SHARJAH

A CIP catalogue record for this title is available from the British Library.

ISBN 9781528928892 (Paperback)
ISBN 9781528928908 (Hardback)

www.austinmacauley.com

First Published (2019)
Austin Macauley Publishers Ltd
25 Canada Square
Canary Wharf
London
E14 5LQ

Chapter One

"God is love,
and anyone who lives in love, lives in God,
and God lives in him." (1 John: 16)

A few years ago, I took part in an Alpha course. During the course of discussion, our group would talk about the God of the Old Testament. This was more a derogatory term, meaning a god who was quick to anger, slow to show compassion, and demanding. How many of us today are walking around with a distorted view of God the Father, the Son and the Holy Spirit? Do we believe in a god and if so, what kind of god do we believe in? Through studying scripture, with the guidance of the Holy Spirit, I have come to have a completely new understanding of the God I worship, the Godhead of the Father, the Son and the Holy Spirit. This is the God I would like to share, the God 'whom my heart loves' (*The Song of Songs* 13:1–2).

The Christian and Jewish religions are the only ones in which we can have a personal relationship with our God. And yet, so often, this is not the case. Somewhere along the way, we can get lost or diverted in spiritual debates, using spiritual jargon, becoming wise in our own opinions, and being totally engrossed or immersed in our own egotistical battles that we cut God out of the picture, or manufacture a God we want. There are even those who use God as, for want of a better word, a 'sugar daddy', a god who will provide for all our material comforts, just so long as we keep in a relationship with him. Sometimes, it is good to sit back and reflect on the key question: 'What is my image of God, if indeed I do have one?'

When we reject the idea of God, are we rejecting a god we have learnt of as a child? Is it one we must live in fear of upsetting; or a God who has such high standards we can never live up to, and is ready to punish us when we fail to reach that expectation; or a wrathful God that must be obeyed without questioning? Recently, I saw a cartoon of Jesus and a young person sitting on a park bench. The question the young man asked Jesus was, "Why do you allow all this suffering in the world, children dying of hunger, families torn apart through war?" Jesus replied, "That is exactly the question I was going to ask you." It is all too easy to shift the blame and responsibility of what is happening in our world today unto an unseen deity, and then to use that image to support our theory that a loving God couldn't exist, as he wouldn't allow suffering to happen. No wonder so many give up and proclaim God didn't create man, man created God!

The evidence of the existence of God is all around us if we but take the time to look and listen and get to know Him. To come to know God is more than just gaining knowledge. Indeed, there is a danger that knowledge is mistaken for wisdom, when in actual fact, wisdom means to be teachable, knowledgeable and skilful. It is an ongoing process but first there must be a desire or want to learn, to find out more, to seek out the truth. After the desire comes the knowledge and then the skill to weave that, which has been learnt, into developing a personal relationship with a God, so filled with love and compassion that He just wants us to come to Him, to grow in our knowledge of Him, and to accept His love. He wants to teach us how to love Him, if we but let Him.

Recently I was at a cancer clinic. It was running very late and the patients were sitting there, totally fed up, all in various stages of the disease. It was a bleak scene when two people met in the corridor, one going into the treatment room, an English girl in her twenties, and the other coming out, an elderly African gentleman. They greeted each other with such love and affection. Apparently, while they were going through their treatment, they had supported one another by praying for each other every day over the phone. When the girl bemoaned the fact that she had done very little for her church since finishing treatment, the man replied, "Aw, don't worry, all people need to know is that God loves them." Their words and love brightened up that dull dismal place. Sometimes, it just doesn't matter where we are or who we are, we just need to hear or be reminded of those words, "God loves you." This is a little phrase every Christian knows, yet what actually does it mean in practice? How does it apply to our lives?

Love is an abstract concept, and thus should be treated as such. To come to an understanding of it, therefore, there is a need to start with the basics, or the concrete. If a six-year-old child came home from school and said, "This week we have been learning about sharing. We put twelve marbles into groups of two, and we had six groups. All of us got it right, and now our teacher says that because we have the right idea, tomorrow we are going to learn about long division," we would react in quite a negative way. Indeed, we would be stunned, and probably absolutely horrified, that such a difficult concept would be introduced at such an early stage, to a child still mastering the basics. However, it doesn't really matter about the age, for even if a child is older, unless they have mastered the basics, they will not be able to apply the concept. All of us recognise that to move from the concrete to the abstract, there must be small simple steps, involving language that is clear and simple, not ambiguous, and especially not with the use of technical terms, and so it should be, when we talk about love and God. If we have an ill-conceived concept of love, or have had a little experience of love in our own lives, how will we be able to understand God's love for us?

However, it is not just our experiences, or ill-formed concepts which can cause a barrier to our understanding of love. In the English language, we have only one word for the feeling, affection, or emotion and that word is 'love'. Unlike the Greek and the Hebrew language, where there are different words for different types of love, we just don't have that. Consequently, the word love is used, overused and misused, to encompass many different degrees of feeling or affection, such as a mother's love, love of food, or of a favourite place. Yes, these meanings of love are important to us, but at different levels. How can we love an inanimate object the same way as a person close to us? In the Hebrew language, there is a solution to this problem as it has several different words that refer to 'love'. They are *ahav*, to love but which also means 'to give'; *dodi*, meaning beloved as of a spousal love; *ra'ha*, brotherly or friendship love, and *racham*, tender mercies, a completed love, or a love that is reciprocated. It is a returned love, it's not all about receiving, there has to be a giving, but we need to experience it, so that when we do, it can do even more than enhance and enrich our lives.

Throughout the Bible, both in the Old Testament and the New Testament, there are countless examples of God's love. "God is love," may be a difficult, abstract concept for us to comprehend, let alone put into practice. However, it is fundamental to our belief and our existence. If God is love, and we are created by God, then we have been created in love. "God created man in His own image; in the image of God He created him," (*Genesis* 1:27). This image is not referring to a physical one. We tend to use such expressions as 'like father like son' or 'he is a chip of the old block' to refer to the way a child is behaving, which is similar to the father, but it is actually his behaviour, his traits which are similar. It is his nature and not his physical resemblance we are referring to, and so it is like God. We are created as a reflection of God's nature, which includes the ability to love. However, when we were created, we were given a free will. We were given the choice to respond to this love or reject it. God cannot force a being he created to love Him, just in the same way we cannot force someone to love us, even someone we have brought into being – our children. Love is a voluntary act, that of giving and receiving. It encompasses so much more than a deep feeling, an emotion. Love is the motivating force in stopping us from becoming hollow and empty. Love is never static; it is a continual process, of growing in knowledge, maturing, evolving and changing. Consequently, it can be a very powerful, life-giving and life-changing force.

Saint Paul understood this when he said, "If I have all the eloquence of men or of angels, but speak without love, I am simply a gong booming or a cymbal clashing" (*1 Corinthians* 13). Indeed, according to Paul, love was the essence, the all-encompassing factor of life, the stability and consistency in which life survives. "If I have the gift of prophecy, understanding all the mysteries there are, and knowing everything, and if I have faith in all its fullness, to move mountains, but without love … it will do me no good whatever" (*1 Corinthians* 13:2–4). Paul goes on to give a simple and easy-to-understand definition of the virtues of love. "Love is always patient and kind, it is never jealous; love is never boastful or conceited; it is never rude or selfish; it does not take offence, and is not resentful. Love takes no pleasure in other people's sins but delights in the truth; it is always ready to excuse, to trust, to hope and to endure whatever comes" (*1 Corinthians* 13:4–7). Thus the presence of love not only affirms others, and in doing so makes them feel lovable and capable, but it also has a very positive effect on our own lives, as it overcomes destructive aspects of our character. It is more than just an emotion, it is a very powerful driving force. So much so that books, songs and films all sell and become popular, and why? The simple answer is because they are based on this one word: 'love'.

There is a common conception that there are two emotions in the world which can be expressed: that of fear and that of love; all the other emotions are nothing more than subcategories of these two. Hence, where there is love, there is positivity, as we may have peace, joy, contentment, serenity and forgiveness. While on the other hand, where there is fear, there is negativity, as we will have anxiety, sadness, depression, fatigue, judgment and guilt. Elisabeth

11

Kübler-Ross, (a Swiss-American psychiatrist) and David Kessler in their book *Life Lessons: Two Experts on Death and Dying Teach Us About the Mysteries of Life and Living,* claim that all positive emotions come from love and all negative emotions from fear. Love cannot survive where there is fear, nor fear where there is love. Consequently, when you don't choose love, you choose fear, as fear and love are incompatible, "There is no fear in love, but perfect love drives out fear" (*1 John* 4:18).

Often in the Bible, there appear to be contradictions, and the use of the word 'fear' would appear to be one of them. Just as we are getting an inkling of this love God has for us, then we come across *Psalm* 147:11, "The Lord delights in those who fear him, who put their hope in his unfailing love," and in *Psalm* 25:14, "The Lord confides in those who fear him; he makes his covenant known to them." As in the word 'love', we have other words that have crept into our vocabulary, which can be open to misinterpretation, misconception, even when used correctly within the context. One such word is 'fear'. The common perception of fear is, as in the definition given by *The English Oxford Living Dictionaries*, 'An unpleasant emotion caused by the threat of danger, pain, or harm.' According to such a definition, how can we love a god whom we have to fear?

When used as 'fear of God', or 'fear of the Lord', fear can take on a completely different meaning. In *Deuteronomy* (10:20), we are told, "It is Yahweh, your God you must fear and serve; cling to Him; in His name, take your oaths." In *Proverbs*, we learn that, "The fear of the Lord is the beginning of wisdom" (9:10). However, the meaning and understanding of fear has changed and become more limited over time. In the past, it was used to encompass more comprehensive meanings. According to the KJV Old Testament Hebrew Lexicon, the Hebrew word for fear is *Yare*, and as in many Hebrew words, there are several meanings for it, such as to stand in awe of, be awed, reverence, honour and respect. Chaim Bentorah, in his book *A Hebrew Teacher Explores the Heart of God through the*

Marriage Ceremony, goes even further and suggests it is so much more than just respect, awe or reverence. He claims that the word used in the Hebrew for *fear,* as in 'fearing God' or 'the fear of the Lord,' is *leyire'ah*. It has nothing to do with dread, or a distressing emotion that originates from concern for one's welfare, but is more concerned with doing what is just and kind in God's eyes, to walk humbly before Him, keep His commandments, and seek unity and oneness with Him. The commandments which are sign posts to keep us going forward in the right direction are just that. Hence, to fear the Lord is more than just keeping the commandments, but being afraid of saying or doing anything that would hurt or wound the heart of God. We need to get to know God so we can avoid hurting or wounding His heart. No wonder the term 'fear of the Lord' is used for the beginning of wisdom!

There is a well-known song with the lyrics, "To know, know, know him, is to love, love, love him." Before we can truly say we love someone, we have to get to know them, to grow in knowledge, first-hand knowledge. Throughout the Bible, both in the Old Testament and the New Testament, there are countless examples of God's words of love and mercy which give an insight into His heart. In the book of Joel, we are called to "Turn to Yahweh your God again, for He is all tenderness and compassion," (Joel 2:13). Micah declared, "Who is a God like you, who pardons sin and forgives the transgression of the remnant of his inheritance? You do not stay angry forever but delight to show mercy. You will again have compassion on us; you will tread our sins underfoot and hurl all our iniquities into the depths of the sea" (*Micah* 7:18–19). Hosea continues the theme of how God responds in love when we return to Him, "I will love them (Israel) with all my heart, for my anger has turned from them. I will fall like dew on Israel. He shall bloom like the lily, and thrust out roots like poplar" (14:5–6), "They will live in my shade; that will grow corn that flourishes, they will cultivate vines" (14:8), "What has Ephrim to do with idols any more when it is I who hear his prayer and care for him? I am like a cypress ever green, all your fruitfulness comes from me" (14:9–10). But perhaps some of the most beautiful examples of God's love and mercy appear in *Isaiah*.

"Do not be afraid, you will not be put to shame, do not be dismayed, you will not be disgraced; for you will forget the shame of your youth and no longer remember the curse of the widow-hood.
For now your creator will be your husband,
His name, Yahweh Sabaoth;
Your redeemer will be the Holy one of Israel,
He is called the God of the whole earth.
Yes, like a forsaken wife, distressed in Spirit, Yahweh calls you back" (Isaiah 54:4–6).
"I did forsake you for a brief moment,
But with great love I will take you back" (Isaiah 54:7–8).
"For the mountains may depart,
The hills be shaken,
But my love for you will never leave you
And my covenant of peace with you will never be shaken" (Isiah 54 4–10).

Just as the Old Testament is filled with God's love for us, so too is the New Testament, where God's unconditional love is made manifest through His son, Jesus, the personification of love. Jesus, who while on earth, explained that His mission was to make the God of love known, "I have made your name known to them and will continue to make it known, so that the love with which you loved me may be in them, and so that I may be in them." (*John* 17:26) Jesus, who came for *all men*, "I have come so they may have life and have it to the full." Jesus, who compared Himself to a shepherd, one who would not only care, protect, nourish, gather-in and lead to new fresh, green pastures but who would willingly give up His life, so His flock could have life. "I am the Good Shepherd: the good shepherd who lays down his life for his sheep" (John 10:11). Jesus, who still reaches out to us with the arms of the cross, ready to gather us in, to bring us back to God, our loving father, into a new and personal relationship with Him.

Throughout the Bible, there are other countless examples of God's works and words which allow us to come into a new and personal relationship with Him. They are there, sometimes obvious, sometimes less so, and consequently it is up to us, to go and find them. Those three little words, "God loves you", so simple yet so meaningful, can be the beginning of an exciting, adventurous journey; one of discovery and intrigue. A pilgrimage to the God of love; a journey that will lead us right into His heart.

Chapter Two

"Israel come back to Yahweh your God; your iniquity was the cause of your downfall. Provide yourself with words and come back to Yahweh" (Hosea 14:2).

It really doesn't matter where we are in our journey in life; if we are at the beginning, middle or coming up to the end, God meets us right where we are. There is a story in Jewish scripture about a rich man and his son who have a falling out. The son leaves home and goes to a distant land. After a time, the rich man sends a servant to find his son and bring him home. When confronted by the servant, the son states that it's impossible to return, as it is too far to come. The father replies to this, by asking the servant to relay the message, "Come as far as you can and I will meet you." This is a very familiar story to Christians. Jesus uses it as the basis for one of the parables 'The Prodigal Son', but embellishes it with more detail. Thus the father, or God, is portrayed not only as a very loving, persistent parent, but also a Father God who is so quick to pardon and takes great joy at welcoming His child back into the fold. All that is required is to turn back and acknowledge His existence, and He will do the rest.

"While he was still a long way off, his father caught sight of his arrival" (*Luke 15*: 20–21). Even before he reached home, his father was already looking for him. Returning to the fold is a common theme in the Old Testament, or to be more precise, a call to return to the fold was the message proclaimed by all the prophets. *Hosea* (14:2–3): "Israel, come back to Yahweh your God; your iniquity was the cause of your downfall." Then in *Hosea* we

16

learn what will happen to those who do return, "I will love them with all my heart, for my anger has turned from them" (14:5–6). In *Isaiah*, we have more of an understanding of this great love but from the feminine nature of God, "Does a woman forget her baby at the breast or fail to cherish the son of her womb? Yet even if these forget, I will never forget you. See I have branded you on the palms of my hand" (49:15–16).

Although the image of branding or engraving on the palms of your hand seems strange, Chaim Bentorah, in his book *The Hebrew Teacher Reveals the Heart of God*, explains that in ancient times it was believed that one's heart was found in one's right hand. Women in the ancient Assyrian Empire, when their sons had reached a certain age and had been inducted into the Assyrian army, would have the son's name tattooed on the right palm. This was a constant reminder of the son who was off fighting a war. According to Assyrian beliefs, that token was as close to her 'heart' as possible. Thus this metaphor helps us to see a God who is so filled with love and longing for our return that He keeps our names permanently close to His heart, carved in His hand.

This portrayal of a father's tender love was continued in the parable of 'The Prodigal son' when Jesus used the phrase 'was moved with pity' (Luke 15:20); not anger, but pity, or as some versions use the word 'compassion', a mixture of both love and pity. The father had witnessed how much the son had suffered, and had lost not only all of his possessions, but also his dignity. Through the son's transgressions, the only people who were hurt and suffered, were actually the son himself, and the father, who had to witness his son's fall from grace within the family. All the father could do was to send a servant to encourage the wayward son to return to him. The most important part of the message was that no matter how far he, the son, had fallen, the father still loved him dearly, wanted him to return so that he could take him in his arms and give him that message, face to face.

There is a beautiful story told of a young couple in the North West coast of the United States. One Christmas Eve they had gone to their holiday cabin up in the mountains. The wife left to go to Midnight Mass and the husband settled himself down in front of a cosy fire with a book. He had just started to read when he heard a bang at the window. He stopped and listened. It happened again. Getting up, he looked outside and saw gulls running around outside on the icy ground. They had had their wings frozen and consequently had flown into the window, unable to fly anymore. Immediately, he went outside to rescue them. He chased after them, desperately trying to catch the frozen birds, so that he could bring them into the heat, thaw out their wings and then release them back out into their environment, where they would be able to survive and fend for themselves. However, the more he tried to reach out and pick them up, the more they scattered. In desperation, he stopped and thought, 'If only I could speak to them in their language then they would listen to me, would understand that I am only trying to help them. Unless they let me approach and help them, they will freeze to death'. Just at that moment, the bells rang out in the valley to signal the beginning of Christmas Eve Mass. As he listened to the peal of the bells, a realisation struck him and he understood the true meaning of Christmas. Jesus is that messenger that God has sent so He can communicate with us in order to help us from stumbling around hurting ourselves, in our cold, frozen state.

When we listen and turn back, and allow God Our Father to help us in our pitiful, vulnerable state, He will do so immediately. In 'The Prodigal Son', we are told that the father '*r*an to his son, *embraced* him and *kissed* him' (Luke 15:20–21). In Biblical times, a rich man would never pick up his robes and run, as it was considered undignified, just was not the etiquette of the day, so by using this example, Jesus is giving us an understanding of a father who is just so overjoyed at a son/daughter returning to him, all transgressions are forgotten. This is an illustration of a

Father who wants to hurry out to meet us, throw his arms around us, pick us up gently, and hold us close to His heart. Thus bringing us back into the heat and letting our wings thaw, so we can lead a full life, free of all the restraints that were hampering us.

God will meet us where we are, as we are. All we need to do is make a little effort and He will do the rest. A good example of this is in the New Testament, in the meeting between Jesus and Zacchaeus (*Luke* 19: 1–10). All Zacchaeus, a wealthy tax collector, wanted to do was catch a glimpse of Jesus. Although small of stature, he still managed to climb a sycamore tree, no mean feat! Imagine his joy and surprise when Jesus not only stopped under the tree, but looked up into his face, and if that was not enough, Jesus called Zacchaeus by name! Poor old Zacchaeus, he must have almost fallen out of that tree with shock! However, when he looked into the face of Jesus, he responded to that call immediately. He had been curious, and had only wanted to catch a glimpse of Jesus, but he received more, oh so much more!

Just like Zacchaeus, we also are called by name. "Do not be afraid, for I have redeemed you. I have called you by your name, you are mine" (*Isaiah* 43:1). Isaiah was a prophet, someone who would bring the word of God to the people, who would be the intermediary between God and His people. The one who normally would have to communicate the heartbreak of the God of love, for the people who had turned away from Him. Indeed, many of their words held doom and gloom. However, if we see a child about to run into the road, we don't say in a quiet voice, "Oh you shouldn't do that." We would shout and probably use imperative language, thus ensuring the child understood the gravity of the situation. So it was with the prophets, they needed to get across the message that if the people continued on their own destructive path, it could only end in tears, they could end up like the frozen gulls. Unfortunately, it seems to be the negative messages we associate with the prophets, messages from an angry god, so it is important to be reminded of the very positive, beautiful words of love that were expressed by the prophets in the Old Testament, and especially Isaiah.

The book of Isaiah, although written about five hundred years before the coming of Jesus, is often referred to as the fifth gospel, as it foretold so much about the life and death of Jesus, the Messiah. Even the verse, "Do not be afraid for I have redeemed you" (43:1), could be seen as a prophecy about the death of Jesus. The word 'redeem' means, according to the Oxford Dictionary, to 'Atone or make amends for (sin, error, or evil), or to save (referring to the act of saving someone) from sin, error or evil'. This is exactly what Jesus did for us, on the cross! He redeemed us. By His death on the cross, He took away all the stumbling blocks, or sins that were preventing us from coming to know God, as a loving Father, Abba. Isaiah is telling us in verse 43:1, we have nothing to fear or worry about. It doesn't matter that we have sinned, hurt God, hurt one another, and indeed even hurt ourselves. God really has taken care of that. All that matters is we understand that He knows us personally, knows us by our name, but more importantly are the words, "You are mine." We belong to Him, like a husband belongs to his wife or vice versa. It is a deep spiritual relationship, one based on God's unconditional love for us.

As in the story of the rich man and his son, or Zacchaeus, all we have to do is make a little effort, to get to know this God of love. We just need to follow up that curiosity, and God will do the rest! No matter what our circumstances, state or belief, God just wants to welcome us back into the fold. The problem that occurs with us is, due to our conditioning within society, we fail to understand the message; that all-important message of unconditional love. "Man is born free yet everywhere he is in chains," Rosseau. Being a part of a society means we are conditioned and restricted from birth, whether it be by limitations or by the expectations that are put upon us. Most of our social learning or conditioning comes from a reward and punishment system. If we are good, we get praise at the least, or a prize at best. However, if we don't follow or do what is expected of us, then punishment will follow, in some form or other. That punishment can be harsh, and it really doesn't matter whether it is in words or in actions.

I remember once, as a young student teacher teaching a class of six-year-olds. In the middle of the lesson, the head teacher walked in to the classroom. One of the pupils, who was quite quiet and withdrawn, ran up to her and proudly held up a picture that he had just completed. She looked at the child and said, in a really stern, disapproving voice, "Your father's a pilot. You can do better than this." As she spoke, the child's expression changed. He looked as though he was going to burst into tears, turned with shoulders sagging and made his way slowly back to his seat. No matter what I said or did, from then until the end of the practice, I couldn't undo the damage that was done to the child's confidence. All of us have similar experiences in our background, especially in our formative years, whether it be in school or at home, that have dented our confidence, made us feel inadequate and in many cases, unlovable. It is our experiences, our interaction, within our own family and within our wider family or society, that has helped create the person we are, and we need to be aware of that. However, we don't have to stay in the 'chains' that others have created for us. Within us we have that ability to change, if we so desire. However, it does mean acknowledging the negativity that has happened in our past and taking the first step and starting off in a new direction.

Every journey undertaken provides a means of change, in one form or another. Even if we start out feeling like a victim, we have that ability to change, if we but have the courage to let go of our security blanket of self-pity. While we are harbouring grievances and apportioning blame on others for our growth and development, indeed where we are at in the present stage of our life, we are going to make very little progress. We need to take back control and be realistic. Blaming people and events in the past, for what is happening in our lives today, is not going to benefit us, not one little bit. Once when I was in a queue, in a well-known store, a group of young people was in front of me. From their accents and their appearance, it would appear their origin was from a Middle-Eastern country. One was wearing a padded jacket, and on the sleeve was a very small square of material. On it were written the words: 'Do not look back, that is not the direction you are going'. What wise words. Sometimes we just have to leave the past, the negative parts of our past, right where it is, in the past.

Indeed the hardest part of moving forward is not looking back. Jesus knew this when He gave similar advice to His early followers, "Once the hand is laid on the plough, no one who looks back is fit for the kingdom of God" (*Luke* 9:62). Harsh words, it would seem, but then it must be remembered that Jesus lived in an agricultural age where His audience would have been very familiar with what 'taking your hand off the plough involved'. For a ploughman to be successful in his work, he *had to* concentrate on the job he started, and the only way forward was not to be distracted by the things left behind. If in the case the ploughman did start to look back, his plough line would become crooked and consequently, the field being ploughed would not yield a full harvest. Jesus was emphasising the importance of commitment, of moving forward, with purpose and determination. Saint Paul also emphasises the importance of looking forward not backwards in his letter to the Church at Phillipi, "All I can say is that I *forget* the past and I strain ahead for what is still for the prize to come. I am racing for the finish, for the prize to which God calls us upwards to receive in Christ Jesus" (4:13–14), and then in a later verse, "Meanwhile, let us go forward on the road that has brought us to where we are" (4:16).

However, our past is important, as it contributes to who we are. Indeed the attitudes and behaviours we witnessed and experienced as children often subconsciously shape the ways we think and act as adults, and we need to be aware of them. So it is important not to bury the past completely. As Jesus said, "When the hand is laid on the plough," meaning once we begin the journey, then it is not a good idea to *keep* looking back. Sometimes, before we begin to move on, we need to stop and confront the past, but in a positive way, because if we don't, it could hinder us on our journey. We could be carrying extra baggage, which could be costly and slow us down. "God doesn't waste anything. You are not defined by your past. You are prepared by your past" (Joel Osteen on Twitter). According to Dodinsky in his book *In the Garden of Thought*, "I do not judge people by the scriptures of their faith, or by the scars of their past, I embrace them for the contents of their hearts." We need to use our past experiences, even our scars, to create new opportunities; to view the negative with a positive; to see not only the good but the possible in every situation. There are so many examples of not only famous people, but of those around us, who have used negativity as a force for positivity, negative comments as a means to produce positive outcomes. There are even those who have used negative school reports as a way of turning their lives around, or has given them the incentive to prove the person wrong. A report from St George's School, Ascot, labelled Churchill as 'naughty' while another report revealed: "He has no ambition. He is a constant trouble to everybody and is always in some scrape or other. He cannot be trusted to behave." Our past can be used in a very positive way to reshape our future, if we but let it and develop the negativity into the positivity.

Another reason for examining our past is that the root of all fears, that which stops us from loving, stems from past experience. These fears, not just phobias, but the fear of abandonment, separation, rejection, of the unknown, to name but a few, need to be acknowledged and confronted. To eradicate them involves firstly being aware of them, identifying them and then tracing them back to their beginnings, their roots. Then just like weeds, they need to be pulled up from their roots and tossed onto the rubbish heap, if we are to truly love ourselves and others. The singer/songwriter John Lennon identified the motivating emotions of love and fear when he wrote, "When we are afraid, we pull back from life. When we are in love, we open to all that life has to offer with passion, excitement and acceptance. We need to learn to love ourselves first, in all our glory and our imperfections. If we cannot love ourselves, we cannot fully open to our ability to love others or our potential to create." Fear can leave us crippled on our journey, can take away our confidence and impede us in learning to love ourselves.

One of the major fears, which many people experience is that of rejection; an irrational fear, based on the assumption that people will not accept us due to our opinions, beliefs, behaviours, background, social class etc. It causes us to build barriers instead of bridges. It impacts on our feelings, making us feel that we are not good enough and that we are a failure. Within relationships, it can cause us to become obsessive, clingy and jealous. It can also destroy relationships that have barely begun through us becoming too serious too soon, which in turn can be a huge deterrent and instead of bringing others closer, drives them away.

If we feel negative about ourselves, rejection can trigger off a number of other feelings. We can start to feel humiliated, lonely, pathetic, not good enough, useless and inadequate. Indeed, we may even feel, in that very negative expression, that 'we are losers'. The more we dwell on these negative feelings, the more pain we're putting ourselves through and the harder it becomes to redress the balance. Indeed the harder it is for us to love ourselves, never mind others. We need to break the negative cycle that has ensnared us, drawn us inward because another danger of the fear of rejection is that it can make us try to fit in, to be one of the gang and in consequence, we are prepared to compromise our views, beliefs and opinions. The desire to be liked and accepted is a powerful driving force not always for the good, which can leave us feeling disillusioned about ourselves and the way in which we lead our lives. Instead of confronting our fears, we ignore them and get carried along with the flow, living our disillusioned life.

In the allegorical novel by Trina Paulus, *Hope for the Flowers*, the main character Stripe, realises early on that there must be 'more to life than just eating leaves', so he looks for a way to get to the sky and discovers himself at the base of a pillar made up of caterpillars, all of them struggling in the same pursuit. He is drawn to them because they are like him, all searching for something more, all disillusioned. On his journey upwards, he meets a companion, Yellow. After a while, Yellow begins to become aware of what is happening around her and feels badly at having to use other caterpillars as stepping stones to reach the top. Stripe also becomes disillusioned, so they leave the pillar together, but then Stripe is drawn back, not only by curiosity but also by wanting to belong and to be accepted by the other caterpillars. He focuses, adapts, and although is aware of the caterpillars he is elbowing out of the way in his quest to get to the top, he isn't deterred. Eventually, he succeeds at being on the top of the caterpillar pillar. This results in disillusionment, as he looks around and discovers many caterpillar pillars, all with caterpillars, similar to himself, trying to get to the top. Then the relevant question is asked, "Is this all there is at the top?" Actually, he has not really achieved his goal to reach the sky; instead, he just has a view of other caterpillars struggling to reach the top of their respective caterpillar pillars. He starts off in a different direction, and starts to descend the pillar, going against the tide. When he reaches the bottom and under Yellow's instructions, he builds a cocoon which allows him to withdraw, change, transform and eventually emerge as a butterfly, beautiful, free from all restraints. And as in all good love stories, he and Yellow, both transformed through love, fly off into the sunset.

Through helping each other and using love as their guide, these two become the greatness that is truly meant for them. They achieved their potential. We are all like Stripe and Yellow on our life's journey. There comes a time when we need to step off the caterpillar pillar, build ourselves a cocoon and transform ourselves into the beautiful lovable human we are meant to be; then we can let go of our fears, our insecurities, accept our inadequacies and learn to love and appreciate ourselves. We need to take time, to look inward, and reflect on all the positive aspects of our character. Even our shortcomings can be used positively, as Saint Paul recognised when he said, "I may not be a polished speech maker," but he did not let that fact deter him; in fact, his words were more powerful because they came from the heart. We tend to be very good at concentrating on our shortcomings but rarely take time to appreciate the beauty within, and to affirm ourselves. We need to stop, look inward, reflect and give ourselves a pat on the back; as the saying goes, "Even a mosquito gets a pat on the back when he is working."

There was another popular saying a few years ago, "God does not create junk." It doesn't matter that we have not, and will never be, on the cover of *Vogue*, be awarded the 'Slimmer of the Year' award, be known for our great wit and intelligence, or have a high social standing. We need to become confident and comfortable within our own bodies, to believe in ourselves. Embedded within us needs to be the belief that we are a beautiful human being, made in God's likeness and no one can take that away from us. We have that ability to love and receive love, and that is all that matters. We need to believe this so we can love ourselves, because if we don't love ourselves, how can we love our neighbours? When asked the most important commandment, Jesus answered, "Love the Lord your God with all your heart and with all your soul and with all your strength and with all your mind"; and, "Love your neighbour *as* yourself" (*Luke* 10:27).

If we don't love ourselves unconditionally, a creation of the God of Love, how can we accept that deep, unconditional love of God our Father? He made us, knows us, cares for us and really, really loves us, just as we are. God's unconditional love, which never fails (*Psalms* 52:8), endures forever (*Psalms* 106:1), and is not motivated by personal gain (*1 John* 3:16).

How can we respond to His call? The call, in the words of the hymn, by Gregory Norbert based on Hosea 14 to,

> *Come back to me,*
> *With all your heart,*
> *Don't let fear*
> *Keep us apart.*

And the reward of our coming back to God the Father is in the response:

> **Long have I waited for**
> **Your coming home to me**
> **And living deeply our new life.**

Through loving ourselves unconditionally, we can come to know, and accept the underserving, unconditional love that God our Father has for each and every single one of us.

Chapter Three

"I lift my eyes to the mountains: where is help to come from? Help comes to me from Yahweh who made heaven and earth" (Psalm 121:1–2).

Perhaps one of the most beautiful examples of God's unconditional love can be found in the Book of Exodus, in the Old Testament. This is a story of a very special journey where God showed His love, patience and compassion; where He provided for His people, every step of the way. Indeed it can provide many lessons for us on our journey.

The story begins with Moses's very touching and beautiful encounter with God. Moses, an Israelite, was brought up by Pharaoh's daughter as an Egyptian prince; he had had to flee Egypt because he had killed an Egyptian, who had been attacking a fellow countryman. It couldn't even be termed self-defence because Moses looked around, 'could see no one in sight, killed the Egyptian and hid him in the sand' (2:11–13). Not even a good lawyer could have got him off a murder charge for that premeditated killing! So Moses had to flee Egypt to Midian, an area of the northwest Arabian Peninsula on the Red Sea. While there, he married the daughter of Jethro, a priest of Midian. Moses, however, stayed attentive to God and we know this because it was while he was driving his father-in-law's flock in the wilderness, he came to 'Horeb, the mountain of God' (3:1), and he saw the burning bush.

In biblical times, it wasn't unusual to see a bush burst into flames, due to the gas and oil that was in the desert, but Moses, being attentive, noticed that although the bush seemed to be blazing, it wasn't being burnt. Being curious, he went to investigate and then God spoke to him and said, "I am the God of your father, the God of Abraham, the God of Isaac and the God of Jacob" (*Exodus* 3:6). Later in verse 13, Moses queries what name he should use when telling the sons of Israel about the encounter, "Then Moses said to God, 'I am to go then, to the sons of Israel and say to them, "The God of your fathers has sent me to you." But if they ask me what his name is, what am I to tell them?'"

In *Exodus* (4:10–11), we learn Moses had a speech impediment. Although there is much disagreement between scholars about what the impediment could be, many agreeing it could have been a stutter, in his book *Hebrew Word Study Beyond The Lexicon*, Chaim Bentorah claims that Moses asked this question because he was thick of tongue and couldn't get his tongue around the names of God, as there were letters he could not pronounce properly; letters in the name Jehovah. God answered him, "I Am who I Am" (Exodus 3:14), or as it would have been originally spoken in Hebrew, 'Yahweh'. This answer could have fulfilled two purposes, one being that the name Yahweh can be said on the exhalation of breath and so does not need the use of the tongue in producing the word. In addition to this, Yahweh is spelt using the Hebrew letters YHVH. Hebrew letters are not the same as letters in the English alphabet. Each letter is a symbol, full of many inner meanings, from the way it is written, and to the position it appears in the Hebrew alphabet. Consequently, the letters have many meanings which can range from the literal to that of a much deeper spiritual meaning.

The first letter of Yahweh is the letter Y, which is the tenth letter of the Hebrew alphabet, and it symbolises the spiritual realm. Of the twenty-two letters of the alphabet, the Y, or *Yod*, is the smallest, barely larger than a dot and is regarded as the most powerful. It is suspended in the air, a reminder to keep looking up to the heavens, "where our help will come from," (*Psalm* 12:1). In *Exodus* (17:11), we learn, "As long as Moses kept his arm raised, Israel had the advantage: when he let his arm fall, the advantage went to the Amalekites." Moses was quite simply reminding the Israelite army of the *Yod*, the beginning letter of Yahweh, and that in the midst of battle, they needed to keep their mind focused on the power and mercy of God, and while they could do that, even in battle, they would become victorious.

The *Hei*, or the fifth letter of the Hebrew alphabet, expresses the idea that God is truly present with us, He is omnipresent. Jesus said in *Matthew* (28:20), "And know that I am with you always: yes, to the end of time." Time as we know it only exists on earth, so when Jesus said this, the Disciples would have been reminded of the *Hei*, but there is also a significant meaning in this letter and that is, although God is always present with us, we need to learn to listen to His voice. Often we may hear people in difficult situations say that they have prayed and they know that God is with them in their situation. True, we do know God is with us, and will answer our prayer, but if we asked for help, then acted in a way to bring about the solution we wanted, or acted through our own desires, then the outcome could be disastrous. So much so that our hearts could become hardened and we turn away from the presence of God because we feel let down by Him. Just as the *Yod* reminds us to keep seeking the face of God, the *Hei* reminds us that we need to learn to listen to the whispers of God. God may not speak as loudly, or dramatically, as He did with Moses, but we can be assured that if we really make the effort to listen, God will surely speak to us, guiding us and revealing His plans, His directions for us. He will listen, but so must we!

In YAVH, we also have the *Vav* and a final *Hei*. The *Vav* is a connection between heaven and earth. The *Vav* teaches us that we can't succeed in our natural world without being united with God. Indeed without God none of our endeavours will be successful, we can't do it under our own steam. The double use of the letter *Hei* means a divine revelation. Thus not only was Moses able to tell the Israelites, *who* spoke to him in the burning bush, he was also able to give them a hidden message in the letters, a reassurance that God was truly in the plan and therefore they would succeed. Moses listened to God and he obeyed His will but he had his doubts.

Moses' main objection to following God's plan was that he didn't consider himself as a leader because of his speech, as he said to Yahweh, "But, my Lord, never in my life have I been a man of eloquence, either before or since you have spoken to your servant. I am a slow speaker and not able to speak well" (*Exodus* 4:10–12). God answered him, perhaps the same answer He gives to us when we feel we are unworthy to follow His calling. "Now go, I shall help you to speak and tell you what to say." Moses believed and trusted completely in God's promises. Even though 'he was the humblest man that had ever lived' (*Numbers* 12:3), Moses spoke out very powerfully when the Egyptians followed the Israelites, to where they were encamped, by the Red Sea.

What a dilemma Moses had! Behind him was the Red Sea, in front the Israelites, "about six hundred thousand – all men – not counting their families. People of various sorts joined them in great numbers; there were flocks, too, and herds in immense droves" (*Exodus* 12:37–38). Behind them was the mighty Egyptian army made up of Pharaoh in his chariot leading "six hundred of the best chariots and all the other chariots in Egypt, each manned by a picked team" (14:7–8). Quite understandably when the Israelites saw the encroaching army, they were terrified and cried out blaming Moses for bringing them into the situation, "Were there no graves in Egypt that you must lead us to die in the wilderness?" (14:11). In the face of such an impossible situation, Moses stood his ground and courageously proclaimed, "Have no fear! Stand firm, and you will see what Yahweh will do to save you today: the Egyptians you see today, you will never see again. Yahweh will do the fighting for you: you have only to keep still" (14:13–14). The Israelites, probably at that stage, felt like lynching Moses but they had no choice; if they wanted to live, they had to look to the heavens and put their trust fully in God, to deliver them from their enemies.

Their trust was rewarded. "Moses stretched out his hand over the sea. Yahweh drove back the sea with a strong easterly wind all night, and he made dry land of the sea. The waters parted and the sons of Israel went on dry ground right into the sea, walls of water to right and to left of them" (Exodus 14:21–23). There was once a speaker at a Christian meeting who was giving a possible theory on how the Israelites could have crossed over on dry land and thus suggesting there was no miracle at all involved. After a lengthy explanation, a little old man at the front of the congregation suddenly jumped up, started to dance around, singing "Praise God, praise God, a miracle, a miracle". At which the speaker stopped and said, quite patiently – perhaps his response may have been different if it hadn't been a religious gathering – "No, no, I have just explained how due to tides etc., the Israelites could have crossed the Red Sea in one foot of water." Back came the reply, "Ah, I wasn't talking about the Israelites; according to your theory, the mighty Egyptian army drowned in one foot of water." We can't have it both ways!

Sometimes, we can be so focused on the Israelites escaping the Egyptian army through the parting of the Red Sea, we can miss the other part of the story, that of the Pharaoh, a proud, powerful, stubborn man. In the Hebrew Bible book of Exodus, Moses and Aaron had set out to try to convince Pharaoh that there is only one God, but Pharaoh refuted their claim, to him there were many gods. The Egyptians, like many pagan cultures, worshiped a wide variety of nature-gods and attributed to their powers the natural phenomena they saw in the world around them. There was a god of the sun, of the river, of childbirth, of crops, etc. Events like the annual flooding of the Nile, which fertilized their croplands, were evidences of their gods' powers and goodwill. So the Pharaoh's reply to Moses's request to let the Israelites go was, "Who is this Lord that I should obey his voice to let Israel go? I know not the Lord, neither will I let Israel go" (*Exodus* 5:2).

Then followed the ten plagues, before each one Moses used the words, "This is what the Lord, the God of the Hebrews, says: Let my people go, so that they may worship me" (*Exodus* 12:2). In retrospect, it would appear that the plagues served to contrast the power of the God of Israel with the Egyptian gods, invalidating them, as several of the plagues could be seen as judgment on specific gods associated with the Nile, fertility and natural phenomena. Two of the most important sources of life for the ancient Egyptians were the Nile River and the Pharaoh. Egyptians perceived that the Nile River made possible the abundant food that was a major source of their well-being.

Therefore in the first plague, there is a real challenge for the Pharaoh. First, the waters of the land of Egypt were to be turned into blood. Unfortunately for the Egyptians, not only the floods of the Nile but all the waters of Egypt, wherever they were, turned to blood. The fish died in the rivers and lakes, and for a whole week, man and beast suffered horrible thirst. After due warning, the Egyptians experienced their second plague. Aaron stretched forth his hand over the waters of Egypt, and frogs, which were highly regarded as an ancient symbol of fertility, related to the annual flooding of the Nile, swarmed forth. They covered every inch of land and entered the houses and bedrooms. The third plague included bugs which crawled forth from the dust to cover the land. When Aaron stretched out his hand with the rod and struck the dust of the ground, lice came upon men and animals. All the dust throughout the land of Egypt became lice (*Exodus* 8:16–17).

The fourth plague to harass the Egyptians consisted of hordes of wild animals roving all over the country, and destroying everything in their path. Then God sent a fatal pestilence that killed most of the domestic animals of the Egyptians. How the people must have grieved when they saw their stately horses, the pride of Egypt, perish; when all the cattle of the fields were stricken at the word of Moses. Boils were the sixth plague sent upon the Egyptians, which were so painful and horrible, and yet the Pharaoh did not relent. He watched his people suffer.

Even when Moses announced that a hailstorm of unprecedented violence was to sweep the land; no living thing, no tree, no herb was to escape its fury unhurt; safety was to be found only in the shelter of the houses; those, therefore, who believed and were afraid might keep in their homes, and drive their cattle into the sheds, still nothing changed. Then followed the ninth plague. For several days all of Egypt was enveloped in a thick and impenetrable veil of darkness which extinguished all lights kindled. However, it is the last plague that all first-born in the land of Egypt, from the first-born of King Pharaoh, down to the first-born of a captive in the dungeon, and all the firstborn of the cattle, died. The firstborn, like the first fruits of the harvest, belonged to God (*Exodus* 13:11–15), so the greatest punishment a family could receive was to lose their first born. In this plague, God struck at the very heart of the nation.

Although sign after sign had been given, waters of the Nile turned into blood (7:14–25), frogs covered the land (7:26–8:15), lice (mosquitoes) attacked their bodies (8:16–19), gadflies invaded the land (8:20–32), the Egyptians' cattle died (9:1–7), boils attacked the Egyptians (9:8–12), hailstorms brought destruction (9:13–35), locusts destroyed the harvest (10:1–20), total darkness for the Egyptians only (10:21–29), the firstborn of Egypt died (11:1–10, 12:29–34) Pharaoh remained absolute in his determination. He had stubbornly refused to let go of his pride, his worshipping of other gods. Although he saw the suffering his people were experiencing, he could not acknowledge the 'Lord, (the One) that I should obey his voice.' Was it fair that the Egyptian people should suffer because of the refusal of their king to admit to the truth of what was happening around them? Let us not lose sight of the fact that the Israelites were being held in slavery, were being abused, were being held in chains – man's inhumanity to man. Was it fair that the first-born had to die for something that was not their fault, for the sin of their Pharaoh? The first-born had a quick death, unlike God's own son, whose violent, undeserved death was for our liberation, our freedom from the slavery of sins that binds us. Sometimes, we too like Pharaoh miss all the signs.

It wasn't until the chariot wheels began to sink into the sand that Pharaoh had that Eureka moment, when the penny dropped. "He so clogged their chariot wheels that they could scarcely make headway. 'Let us flee from the Israelites,' the Egyptians cried, 'Yahweh is fighting for them against the Egyptians!'" (*Exodus* 14:25–26). Pharaoh had recognised the one true God. If at that moment he had called on Yahweh the God of mercy, both he and his army would have been saved.

All Pharaoh needed to do at that moment was to forget his pride and humility, and cry out, "Be *merciful* unto me, O *God*, be *merciful*" (*Psalm* 57). The Lord would have met him right where he was and forgiven him, and saved not only him but his army. We know this because there are countless examples of God's mercy and forgiveness, throughout the ages.

This mercy or tender loving forgiveness of God is something the Psalmist knew well. The book of Psalms contains many wonderful verses about mercy, love and hope. 'Mercy' is often used when talking about God's love and care over us. One definition of mercy is God withholding the punishment we deserve, "For You, Lord, are good, and ready to forgive, and abundant in loving kindness to *all* who call upon You" (*Psalm* 86:5). "The Lord is good to everyone. He showers compassion on *all* his creation" (*Psalm* 145: 9). David, in *Psalm* 32, praises God for his mercy, which is underserved:

"Happy the man whose fault is forgiven, whose sin is blotted out (32:1);
All the time I kept silent, my bones were wasting away with groans, day in and day out (32:3);
At last I admitted to you I had sinned; no longer concealing my guilt,

I said, I will go to Yahweh
And confess my fault.
And you, you have forgiven the wrong I did, have
pardoned my sin.
That is why each of your servant prays to you
in time of trouble" (32:5–6).

It wasn't only The Psalmist who recognised God's forgiveness and mercy. Even Jonah, a reluctant prophet, understood that God was tender-hearted, slow to punish and quick to forgive. God had directed Jonah to go to the wicked city of Nineveh to deliver God's message that the people there needed to repent and turn away from their sins. Although Jonah tried to avoid the mission, he did eventually deliver the message. "Then the people of Nineveh believed in God; and they called a fast and put on sackcloth from the greatest to the least of them" (3:5). However, poor old Jonah was a little peeved with God, "Jonah was very indignant; he fell into a rage. He prayed to the Lord and said, 'Ah! Lord, is not this just as I said would happen when I was still at home? That was why I went and fled to Tarsish: *I knew that you were a God of tenderness and compassion, slow to anger, rich in graciousness relenting from evil"* (4:1–11). However, Nineveh's repentance must have been short-lived; it was destroyed in 612 BC.

Not only was Ninaveh's repentance short-lived but so too was the Israelites. Even though God rescued them, saved them, fed them, even lead them, "God gave them the pillar of *cloud by day* to lead them in the way He wanted them to go and the pillar of *fire by night* to give light" (*Exodus* 13:21–22), they still turned to other gods. Turning to other gods meant so much than just simply bowing down to an idol. One of the Egyptian, and consequently Canaanite god, was Moloch, or Baal Hammon, the god associated with child sacrifices. Worshippers of this god would sacrifice children in times of great distress. Indeed, it was seen as a form of abortion, of getting rid of unwanted children. Altars to Baal would have an area beside them for musicians, so that their playing would drown out the cries of the children, as they were being sacrificed. When they didn't want to sacrifice their own children but wanted Baal to show them favour, or sometimes in desperation, they would buy children for the purpose of sacrifice or even to raise servant children, instead of offering up their own.

The Israelites, although they had experienced first-hand the power of God throughout their years in the wilderness, often turned to these other gods and turned their backs on the God who loved them. They were like Hosea's unfaithful wife Gomer, whom God likens to His relationship with Israel, she breaks Hosea's heart but each time Hosea takes her back, just like God does with us. "That is why I am going to lure her and lead her out into the wilderness and speak to her heart. I am going to give her back her vineyards, and make the Valley of Achor a gateway of hope. There she will respond to me as she did when she was young, as she did when she came out of the land of Egypt" (*Hosea* 2:16–18).

These are *not* the words of an angry God, *nor* a vengeful God, but a vulnerable God, who is like a husband prepared to welcome back into the marriage his unfaithful wife, with open arms and a heart filled with love and forgiveness. Even if we do go of after other gods, we only have to turn back to him in humility, and unlike Pharaoh, to let Him change our stubborn hearts, so we can acknowledge His love and He will welcome us back with open arms. We just need that reminder to keep looking up, to seek Him, to look for directions and to learn to listen to Him.

There are countless lessons to be learnt from the story of the exodus of the Israelites out of Egypt, not only that of the signs all around us of a God, who is not only with us on our journey, but who may actually initiate it, and is with us every step of the way. It is also really important, in the story of the Exodus, to see the message that is being given. God never breaks His promises. He had promised Moses that He would "Free you of the burdens which the Egyptians lay before you; release you from slavery; with strokes of power

I will deliver you; adopt you as my own people; be your God; bring you to the land I swore I would give to Abraham, Isaac and Jacob; give this land to you for your inheritance" (Exodus 6:6–8). Even after all God had done for them, had kept His promises to them, the Israelites often forgot how God loved them unconditionally, cared and protected them. The Israelites spent a long time in the wilderness, wandering aimlessly, looking inward and around them but forgetting to look up in trust, for direction to a God who really loved them and cared about them. A gentle loving Father, who was leading them on a journey of not only self-discovery, but during their time in the wilderness was revealing Himself to them every step of the way.

Chapter Four

"If only you would listen to him today,
Do not harden your hearts as at Meribah.
As you did that day in the wilderness,
when your ancestors challenged me, tested me,
although they had seen what I could do"
(Psalm 95:8–9).

Throughout our journey, it is important to keep looking upward, however, we must also spend time looking inward. Unlike the Israelites, we need to get the balance right. If we don't, we may miss what is actually happening within ourselves, within our hearts. If we don't, without us even realising, our hearts may become hardened.

Every now and again, I will come across something which I didn't even realise was in the Bible. One such example was, "I know your deeds, that you are neither cold nor hot. I wish you were either one or the other!" (*Revelations* 3:15–16). At first, when reading it, I thought of what one priest once called 'the insurance Catholics'. They weren't sure if there was a God or not, but came along to Mass every Sunday just in case there was, so that when they died, 'they were covered'. Then I stumbled across, in *Luke* (1:5–23), the story of the appearance of the Angel Gabriel announcing the good news to Zachariah, that God had heard his prayers and granted him the desire of his heart. He was going to become a father. This son would become known as John the Baptist. Now Zachariah was a very holy religious man, or so it would appear.

Zachariah belonged to the Abijah section of the priesthood, his wife Elizabeth was a descendent of Aaron. "Both were worthy in the sight of God, and scrupulously observed all the commandments and observances of the Lord" (*Luke* 1:6–7). While carrying out his priestly duties, of burning incense, an angel of the Lord appeared to him. His reaction left a lot to be desired! First he was disturbed, then he was overcome with fear. However, it was his words that really give an insight into his heart. When the Angel Gabriel had finished telling him that God had heard his prayer and his wife Elizabeth would bear a son, his reply was, "How can I be sure of this?" Why did he say this? His following words give us a clue. "I am an old man and my wife is getting on in years" (*Luke* 1:18). In other words, well, He (God) has left it a bit late. I'm too old and have you seen my wife? She's no spring chicken! Obviously, the words spoken by the Angel Gabriel, "Do not be afraid, your prayer has been heard," touched a raw nerve. Was Zachariah's totally unexpected response filled with bitterness and resentment towards God because He had not answered his prayers? After all, Zachariah must have had to listen, throughout the years, to many accounts of prayers being answered, and even worse, to those people who didn't even serve God, certainly not in the way Zachariah served Him. Perhaps he had just become impatient waiting for the Lord to act, and when he didn't see an answer to his prayer, hardened his heart towards God. Quite ironically, the name 'Zachariah' means 'God remembered!'

Whatever the reason, due to his reaction, Zachariah was struck dumb, "You will have be silenced and have no power of speech" (*Luke* 1:20). Although his punishment for his words at first may seem harsh and undeserving, it can also be viewed in a very positive spiritual way. The following period for Zachariah could be termed, according to the poem of St John of the Cross, 'the long night', or as later became known as 'the long night of the soul', a time for deep reflection, on that which separates us from the love of God. Being struck dumb and not being able to communicate

40

thoughts, words, beliefs, or ideas, can prove to be a very humbling experience. Not only is speech used as a way to express our needs, our desires, our feelings, our innermost thoughts, but it is also a way to show off our intellect, impress others, and certainly in Zachariah's case, a means in which he could establish and maintain his position in society. At that time, it was a great honour for a priest to burn incense in the temple, no priest was allowed the honour more than once in his life time, and indeed many were never chosen at all.

Zachariah therefore when he lost his speech, went from a respected Jewish priest to one who was humbled, he wasn't even consulted over his son's name. "On the eighth day, they came to circumcise the child; *they* (the Holy Men in the Temple) were going to call him Zachariah after his father but his mother spoke up" (*Luke* 1:59–60). Although Elizabeth spoke, *they* ignored her, didn't even listen to her and it was only then that they made signs at Zachariah, who responded by indicating he needed to communicate through writing so, 'a writing tablet' was brought to him and he 'wrote'; "His name is John" (*Luke* 1:63). Through his long period of being unable to communicate, he had learnt not only to listen to God but to obey him, the sin that had separated them was no more. "At that instant, his power of speech returned and he spoke and praised God" (1:63–64). When his speech returned, the first thing Zachariah did was to offer his heartfelt thanks and admiration of God, possibly not only for his speech returning but also for the silent, reflective period that saw him, like the prodigal son, look inward, and become aware of that which had cut him off from the love of God, of the Father. He had been going through his priestly duties, possibly carrying them out very well, yet he had stopped in his spiritual journey. He needed time to be reflective, to become aware of his true feelings, indeed come to terms with his situation and return to the love of God his Father.

There are times when we too, like Zachariah, need to examine our relationship with God. Do we also get impatient when our prayers are not answered instantly? Do we become inwardly lukewarm when other people's prayers are answered, and God forbid, even those who we consider to be a lot less spiritual than us? We too may feel our prayers should be answered because we have spent a long time in church, just as Zachariah spent a lot of time in the temple. Perhaps we see God as a type of sugar daddy; we keep him sweet through praying to him, and in return, he gives us whatever we desire!

To help answer these questions, we must first decide on our perception of prayer. In *Matthew* (7:7), we are told, "You have not because you ask not." The point is, God wants us to ask for our heart's desire. "Ask and it shall be given to you; search, and you will find; knock and the door will be opened to you. For the one who asks *always* receives, the one who searches *always* finds, the one who knocks will *always* have the door opened to him" Matthew (7:7–9). As one priest in his sermon on prayer said, "Be careful what you ask for in prayer!" Our prayers are very powerful! We know our prayers are answered the minute we ask them, however, God's timing and our timing is different. We are so used to living in a society where everything is instant, whether it be coffee or looking and chatting to a person in a different country, it is not surprising we want our prayers to be answered as soon as they are said. We have to just believe and not become impatient. Learning to wait for our prayers to be answered also teaches us to trust. In addition to this, we must remember that God is not giving us an open cheque book!

"Is there a man among you who would hand his son a stone when he asked for bread? Or would he hand him a snake when he asked for a fish? If you then, who are evil, know how to give your children what is good, how much more will your Father in heaven give good things to those who ask him!" (*Matthew* (7:9–11). Luke in chapter 11:13:9–13, echoes Matthew, but instead of the more general expression 'good things', talks about the 'Holy spirit'. In both accounts, however, is the Jesus' assurance, that prayer, if persisted in, would always be heard and granted, and there is the all-important limitation that the thing prayed for must be something 'good' in the eyes of the heavenly Father.

The word 'good', when used in this context, could be argued about, as indeed what we are asking for meets our needs then why is it not good? However, winning the lottery may seem like an answer to prayer, and it may initially take care of money problems but is that the best for us in the long run? As many, many lottery winners will tell you, it may change your life, but not always for the better. Many requests may be made by us for purely selfish reasons which, if granted, would be harmful rather than a blessing to us! Perhaps the best way to describe 'good' is in the Hebrew word *tov*, which means to be in harmony with God. So instead of going to God in prayer and telling Him what we want, we instead use prayer to tell Him our needs and then expect Him to provide. We don't know what is best for us, He does! Sometimes we can look back and see we have been given a lot more than we asked for, or what we asked for was not 'good' for us at the time, but was answered in a completely different way. Sometimes we just ask for the wrong things.

In the school where I began my teaching career, a group of Year Six students would meet, under supervision, every Monday for a time of prayer. One Monday, the person who led the group couldn't make it, so I was asked to stand in for her. Not long after we had started, one of the girls asked me if we could pray for Paddy, as he had been knocked down at the weekend and had died. I led a prayer asking God to welcome Paddy into his kingdom, then stopped and explained it was really important to pray also for the relatives. The girl gave me a strange look, shook her head and explained that Paddy had no relatives. Just as I was thinking, *This is getting worse by the minute,* she exclaimed, "Paddy's a horse!"

We don't always get the prayers right, indeed we don't often use the right words. How then should we pray? Jesus gives us the answers to that question in Luke's gospel, (6:7–

8). "Do not babble as the pagans do, for they think that by using many words, they will make themselves heard. Do not be like them; your father knows what you need before you ask it." Then Jesus gives us a model of what true prayer should be like in what has now become known as The Lord's Prayer. It gives us the framework of how prayer should be composed.

Interesting, in the beginning of the 'Our Father', the first four lines are similar to the first three commandments, or the signposts to keep us on the right path of our journey. They are about putting God first. The opening of the prayer, "Our Father," teaches us to whom our prayers are to be addressed, straight to God the Father. In calling him 'Our Father', we acknowledge not only our relationship to him, but our dependency on him, we need Him. "Hallowed be your name" is telling us to worship God, and to praise Him for who He is, for His power, His glory, His compassion, His approachability. The phrase "your kingdom come, your will be done on earth as it is in heaven" is a reminder to us that we are to pray for God's plan in our lives and the world, not our own plan. We are to pray for God's will to be done, not for our desires. We are looking to Him for direction and guidance. This phrase is like a bridge, a connection between heaven and earth, connecting God the Father and us. The emphasis is now on our needs. We are encouraged to ask God for the things we need in the words, "Give us today our daily bread. And forgive us our debts, as we have forgiven those who are in debt to us" reminds us to not only confess or be aware of our sins, our failings, ours fears but to turn from them. When we forgive others, we let go of the hurts and pains they have caused us. In the same way as God has forgiven us, or washed away all evidence of our sinfulness. The conclusion of the Lord's Prayer, "And lead us not into temptation, but deliver us from the evil one" is a plea, a call for help to stop us stumbling around in the dark, turning away from God and falling into sin. It is a request for protection from the attacks of the devil, or the evil one.

The Lord's Prayer is an example of how we should be praying given to us by Jesus. It was how He spoke to His Father so how can we go wrong when we recite it? Indeed, this is exactly the advice Jesus offers to us, just keep it simple and pray straight from the heart. God is far more interested in our communicating with Him and speaking from our hearts than He is in the specific words we use. Indeed, sometimes we don't even need words, as the second example of how we should pray appeared in Luke's Gospel (7:11–17).

Jesus was on his way to Jerusalem from Nazareth, accompanied by his disciples and a great number of people when he came to a town called Naim. At the gate of the town, he met a funeral procession, that of the only son of a widow. When Jesus saw her, he felt sorry for her, went up to her and said, "Do not cry" (7:13), These were the only words spoken, so gentle and so humble, as Jesus said, "Learn from me for I am gentle and humble in heart" (*Matthew* 11:29). Indeed these words, 'do not cry', were the only words needed to make the woman look up; up out of her grief. The phrase bowed down with grief is so true. Grief, the emotional reaction to loss, can be crippling, leaving those experiencing it filled with fear, anxiety and over-burden. Grief or grieving caused by death should never be underestimated, as it involves loss, not only that of a loved one and best friend but may also be the loss of a life style, security, finance to name but a few.

The widow woman of Naim had not only lost her husband but had also lost her only son, her provider; her world must have fallen apart at the son's death. Just for one split second she looked up, out of the darkness and misery that was surrounding her, and what did she see? A face so filled with love and compassion, someone looking into her eyes; the eyes, the gateway of the soul. In Jesus' presence, she let him look right into her pain, misery, her shattered life. In return, Jesus then "went up and put his hand on the bier and the bearers stood still, and he said, 'Young man I tell you to get up.' And the dead man sat up and began to talk." The simple words of command were sufficient to bring him back to life. For the second time in the story, only a few words were used, were needed. He knows us, knows what's in our hearts so all we need to do is come into his presence, look up into his face, a face so filled with compassion, and let Him see what is in our hearts, and He will not disappoint us.

There is also something we can be assured of and that is, it doesn't matter what words we use, indeed if any, there is a certain prayers that will get an immediate response. And that is the one when we are seeking and ask to get to know Him (God) better. We can ask it through His son Jesus, by saying the simple prayer, "Lord I want to get to know you better," or just simply, "Jesus, help me to know you," because as Jesus said, "If you really know me, you will know my Father as well" (*John* 14:7).

Another thing we can be sure about when praying is that when we pray as a group, church or spiritual body, we will get it right. Jesus is there with us, "I tell you solemnly once again, if two of you on earth agree to ask anything at all, it will be granted to you by my father in heaven. For where two or three meet in my name, I shall be there with them" (*Matthew* 18: 19–20). If only we truly believed these words, how powerful our prayers for peace, reconciliation, conversion of hearts etc. could be when we pray them, not only as a church or spiritual body, but also just where a few believers are gathered in prayer. However, it is important to remember that a Christian cannot stand alone, we need each other; we need to belong to a group of fellow believers, not only to support one another on our spiritual journey but also how much more effective our prayers can when we join with others asking the Father that all, whatever nationality, race, religion, or colour, may be able to live in peace and harmony with dignity.

Not only do we need to look upwards and inwards but we must also look around us, be attentive to what is happening, in our parish, community, neighbourhood, and even in the world. When we look around us, we become aware of problems, and much suffering which involves our fellow human beings. Instead of feeling helpless, we can pray that their suffering may be alleviated. Instead of feeling helpless, we can do something positive and consequently help to take a more active role in helping to bring about peace, harmony and reconciliation. Instead of bemoaning a God who allows wars and evil to happen, we could join Him in the battle, using the sword of prayer, to bring about peace, and help spread His love.

Indeed not only do we not listen but we also, at times, get in the way, in our endeavour to do 'God's work, or spread His word'. When out walking with my newly-born twins, a woman stopped and asked the usual question, "Twins?" My sixteen-month-old son looked up at her and said, "Two babies." Immediately, she stopped looking at the twins, looked at him and said, "How clever," leant down and started talking to him. She was right, he was being clever but not for the reason she was thinking of, because of the words that he had spoken. If people had looked into the pram and said, "Six bananas," that's exactly what my son would have said that day, because that is the way children learn to speak, they repeat language. However, what he had done, in a very subtle way was draw the attention away from the twins and onto himself. That was the clever part!

Without realising it, this is something we often can be guilty of doing, drawing the attention away from God unto ourselves. I was quite shocked when I found myself doing exactly this. When a person had a real answer to prayer, I remarked that I had been praying for her, justifying this by saying to myself, "Well it's important she knows that people have supported her, and God has heard her prayer." What I was actually doing was saying, "God has answered your prayer because I asked Him to, because He and I are so close. He always listens to me." I was right in there taking the credit! Instead of directing her eyes upwards, to the heavens where her help had come from, I was standing in the way, hoping in a very subtle way, that she would see the 'halo'. Of course it is really important to tell people that you will pray for them, or that you are praying for them, especially when they are tell you they are facing any kind of test or trail, sometimes it's the only words of comfort we can offer. However, when there is an answer to prayer, then all we need to do is direct the glory back to God, by simply saying, "God is so good," or "God always listens to us, and gives us our heart's desire. He knows what we need even before we ask." Sometimes, we just need to cut out the middle man!

Basically, we just need to get the balance right. We need to take time to look upward; we need to take time to look around us; we need to take time to look inward, to reflect on our actions and words. With the help of the Holy Spirit, we can listen to the voice of God, for He will speak to us and help us see what is in our hearts, He will lead us and guide us. He can shine a light into our darkest areas, and so melt our hearts with his love. He can soften our hardened hearts with His tender words of love, if only we could learn to listen to Him.

How much more effective our prayers can be if we pray in accordance with God's will and to do so, we have to learn to listen to His voice. Both in the Old Testament and the New, there are numerous references to the importance of listening and responding to God's voice. "My sheep, hear my voice, and I know them, and they follow me" (*John* 10:27–28). "And he said to them, 'Pay attention to what you hear: with the measure you use, it will be measured to you, and still more will be added to you.'" (*Mark* 4:24). In *Revelations* (3:20), "Behold, I stand at the door and knock. If anyone hears my voice and opens the door, I will come in to him and eat with him, and he with me." "So faith" (the substance of your positive imagination and the evidence of things not seen) "comes from hearing, and hearing through the word of Christ" (*Romans* 10:17). How can we do God's will or pray in accordance with His will if we don't learn to listen to Him speaking in our hearts?

Chapter Five

"Anyone with ears to hear should listen and understand."
Mark 4:9. (New Living Translation)

Throughout the Old and New Testament, there are numerous examples of God communicating with His people, some quite dramatic, as in the story of Moses and some less so, as in the case of Elijah, "After the earthquake came a fire, but the LORD was not in the fire. And after the fire came a gentle whisper" (*1 Kings*: 19–12). Our God is a God who communicates with us if we would only listen. In all of the books of the Bible, both the Old and the New Testament, we are constantly being called to 'listen', or as the dictionary definition gives, make an *effort* to hear something; be alert and *ready* to hear something. Jesus explains this further when He says, "If anyone has ears to hear, let him listen" (*Matthew* 11:15). Jesus' simple request is that we use our God-given faculties (eyes to see, ears to hear) to be *ready* to tune in to His words (*John* 10:27–28; *Mark* 4:24; *Revelation* 3:20), to be on the alert, to play close attention to the specifics. "For whatever is hidden is meant to be disclosed, and whatever is concealed is meant to be brought out into the open" (*Mark* 4:22).

On hearing the word, we are meant to do something with it, to help us to come to a deeper understanding, to a deeper knowledge of God. The Chinese have a proverb: 'I hear, I forget; I see, I remember; I do, I understand'. Therefore, to help us understand what is being revealed to us, we need to actively engage in the Word, to mediate on it, make connections, and use it to help us lead a life which will involve loving God and loving others, as ourselves. In the parable of the wise man, Jesus explains the importance of both listening and obeying, or putting into action words heard by comparing it to a wise man setting down firm foundations. "Everyone who comes to me and *listens to my words*, **and** *acts on them,* will be like the man who when he built his house dug, and dug deep, and laid the foundation on rock; when the river was in flood it bore down on that house but could not shake it, it was so well built" (*Luke* 6:47–49).

Where will we hear the word? Quite simply, there are many ways God speaks to us, but first and foremost, God speaks to us through the Bible. The name bible comes from the Latin *biblia*, meaning 'the books' as it contains the contributions of many different authors, over a period of time and it is in these books that God makes Himself known in a wide diversity of ways. Our God is a talking God, He communicates with us in many ways; reveals himself to us. Indeed the word 'revelation' can be understood as being either passive or active. It is either the *activity*, whereby God reveals himself or the substance of that disclosure. Where God reveals Himself in speech, the active sense is used, it is God making himself known in words, while the passive sense focuses on the words themselves; it is where He reveals himself to us, the hidden message that is being conveyed.

Therefore, just like any great classic, the Bible is multifaceted, has many different layers, has many different depths and has to be treated as such. Just like reading Shakespeare, it is not a book that can be just picked up and read, from cover to cover; to do so means we miss the hidden meanings, where God reveals himself to us. Parables, types of analogy, and metaphors are used extensively throughout the Bible as a use of imagery to aid our understanding of God's love, especially in the *Psalms*. In *Psalm* 91, what a beautiful, powerful picture of God as a gentle, loving caring protector is created in verses 3–6, saving us from all dangers, our fears that would encapsulate us:

"He rescues you from the snares
Of fowlers hoping to destroy you;
He covers you with his feathers,
and you shall find shelter underneath his wings.
You need not feat the terrors of night, the arrow that
flies in daytime,
The plague that stalks in the dark, the scourge that
wreaks havoc in daylight."

But perhaps the most beautiful use of metaphors occurs in the poetic book *The Song of Songs*, also known as the *Song of Solomon*. The introduction calls the poem 'the song of songs', a construction commonly used in Scriptural Hebrew to show something as the greatest and most beautiful of its class (as in Holy of Holies). The *Song of Songs* is often referred to as the poem of love, as it is based on married love, and claimed by scholars to be superior to all other love poetry. Indeed many scholars are of the belief that it is describing our relationship with God.

"I hear my Beloved.
See how he comes
Leaping on the mountains, bounding over the hills.
My Beloved is like a gazelle, like a young stag" (The *Song of Songs1:8–9).*

Powerful images about love are given throughout the Bible, in stories, poems and deeds. Even by using our tools of interpretation, while drawing on meaning from the context in which it is written, and using skills of inferencing, with the aid of metaphors and parables, it just is not enough. We may come to an understanding but to fully understand what God is trying to convey to us, we need a guide, a helper, to transform those words from our heads to our hearts. We need to go off, take time to reflect and allow the Holy Spirit to show us the deeper meaning.

Jesus gave us an example, in *Matthew* 14, of how we need to take time, and reflect, and with the help of others to help us, come to a deeper spiritual understanding. After the feeding of the five thousand, we are told, "Directly after this he made the disciples get into the boat and go ahead to the other side while he would send the crowds away." Jesus had send the disciples off 'immediately' after the miracle of the loaves and fishes. Instead of being distracted, he had given them the opportunity to reflect and think about what had just happened. Jesus had used the technique that is now so popular in schools, i.e. talk to your partner, explain what you think this means, or what have you learnt by this; what is it showing; what does it actually tell us? He sent them off as a group, to ponder, discuss and reflect on the miracle of the loaves and fishes.

However, they had got caught up with rowing out into the lake and then were distracted by the wind. (14:22) "When evening came, he was there alone, while the boat, by now far out on the lake, *was battling with a heavy sea*, for there was a head wind" (14:23–24). The keywords here that showed the reaction of the disciples were "*was battling* with a heavy sea". Why personification? Why was the boat battling with the sea? The boat struggled, or 'was battling', could be seen as a collective noun for the people within the boat; they struggled to understand the meaning of the miracle, as they were so caught up in what was happening around them. The disciples had allowed the threatening circumstances around them to deflect from their mission, their understanding.

There could also be another connection with the phrase '*was battling with a heavy sea,*' as it was used only in Matthew's gospel, and he is the only evangelist to use the word 'church'. It could also apply to today, how we collectively, as a church, are constantly faced with raging storms which can rock us and even threaten our existence. Throughout the ages, churches have had to face scandal after scandal. Just like the disciples, there are those who even when they belong to a church, "May see and see again, but not perceive; may hear and hear again, but not understand, otherwise they might be converted and understand" (*Mark* 4:12).

Just like the disciples in the boat, we too can 'struggle' to understand the significance of God's revelations of love. Through the storms that occur around us, and within us, we too can get distracted, thrown off course. Indeed, Jewish Scripture teaches, 'the greater the sage, the greater the evil inclination', and warns us to be aware that as we approach the light, there is a shadow behind us. Our hearts need to be converted and we need time, away from the storms that threaten to engulf us to ponder on the word of God, and allow God speak to us through His scriptures. When we listen, God will speak to us very powerfully through the scriptures.

At a different place and different time, God spoke to me through the same scripture reading, *Matthew 14*: 22–33. I had applied to go and teach in Canada, but when the application was in the early stages, I needed to hand in my notice. Basically, I was leaving a well-paid job where I had received promotion to uncertainty, no guarantee of a job. At that time, I was teaching ten- to eleven-year-olds and each morning I would read a passage from the Bible, then we would think about it, and compose our own prayer. This morning, after resigning, I eventually got to the class and just picked up the Bible. It fell open at *Matthew* 14:22, Jesus walking on the water. "In the fourth watch of the night, he went towards them, walking on the lake, and when the disciples saw him walking on the lake, they were terrified. 'It is a ghost,' they said, and cried out in fear. But at once, Jesus called out to them, saying 'Courage! It is I! Do not be afraid.'" As I read these words, I almost dropped the Bible. I felt Jesus was saying these words to me, God was actually talking to me. That was it! I was in line for a sainthood! Although a practising Catholic all my life, I had never known that God spoke to us directly through the Bible (if we but listen).

Amazed, I looked up but all faces were turned towards me, waiting for me to continue so I read on, "Peter got out of the boat and started walking towards Jesus across the water, but as soon as he felt the force of the wind, he took fright and began to sink. 'Lord save me!' he cried. Jesus put *out his hand at once* and *held him*" (14:31). That was it, I knew what I had to do. I had to keep my eyes focused on Jesus, to step out of that boat, that security, into an unknown situation, I had to step out and walk in faith. Not only that but to continue my journey, I needed to walk in that faith, that complete trust and confidence, to keep focusing on the face of Jesus, especially when the situation could become tempestuous. However, how reassuring to know that when we fail, start to sink, *immediately* Jesus will put out his hand and hold us tightly, allowing us to cling to Him, helping us to continue that walk and not sink, if only we are looking at him, not around us, behind us, but at Him.

God will speak to us through the Bible but if we learn to listen to His voice, He will talk to us in many different ways, we just need to open our eyes and our ears. Perhaps one of the most frequently asked questions on this topic, and especially by new Christians, is: "How do I know when God is talking to me?" Well, if someone comes up to you and says, "I feel the Lord just spoke to me and he said, 'you idiot, that was a stupid thing to do,'" you can reassure them that it certainly wasn't the Lord, just not his kind of language! I know this because I learnt the hard way. I once went through a period of doubting the way I prayed. When I prayed, did I pray in trust, was I really trusting the Lord? Sometimes it felt as though I was handing over my problems with the right hand while taking them back with the left one. It was during this period that the Lord taught me a lesson on listening and on trust, one I was unlikely ever to forget!

Each day, when able, I would go for a walk around the local park. One morning, it was so foggy; I decided I would wait until later. However at noon, it was still foggy but I decided to go anyway. All the way around the park it was eerily silent. My normal routine involved, at a particular part of the park, leaving the path and walking up a slight incline, then along a small wooded area which would lead me back to the main path again. Just as I was coming up to the area, I began to doubt the sensibility of going off into a secluded area, when I suddenly heard footsteps behind me. All I could hear in the stillness were these footsteps, hurrying, getting louder and louder, closer and closer. It was like a scene from the Margery Allingham novel *The Tiger in the Smoke*.

Now the sensible thing would have been to stop and look around; after all, anyone intending to cause harm would sneak up quietly, not announcing their presence nosily? So what did I do? I started to pray a prayer about trusting God. After all, each day I prayed for protection, so now was the time to call in the favour. I said something silly to the effect that I trusted in His protection and I knew He would keep me safe. Still praying, I turned off the path and as I was going up the incline, I disturbed a woodpigeon. Without any warning, the pigeon flew over my right shoulder. I leapt into the air, landed with my heart pounding and then I heard the words, "Do not put the Lord your God to the test." All I could think of saying was, "Lord, I'm sorry and please don't think I am complaining but next time you want to teach me a lesson, could you use a smaller bird, like a robin?"

About ten months later, I woke up to a very wet day. Again I went for my walk at noon, and yet again it was eerily silent, not another person was in the park. As I was coming up to the part of the path where I needed to turn off, I laughed and said, "Alright Lord, I won't put you to the test today. Look, I am taking all necessary precautions, stopping, looking around etc." Then as I walked along the wooded part, I noticed at least five robins flying across my path. Immediately, I thought it was strange, as I had never seen so many robins in this area before, but that was nothing to what I was to see when I left the wooded area and went back onto the main path! There coming waddling down the hill were two Canadian geese. Rarely did the geese visit the park, but this was the first and last time I had actually seen them waking down the hill towards me. Just as I was approaching them, they moved off the path. Cautiously, I went to walk past and as I did, one of them flew right across me into the pond, the wingspan almost hitting me. Immediately, I jumped back and although I was aware they were there, it did give me quite a scare, not only that but I was also puzzled. Then I got it! I almost laughed out loud as I said, "OK, Lord, I get it. If you had used the robins that day to give me a message, I wouldn't have taken any notice as they were too small but if you had used the Canadian geese, then I would probably have died of a heart attack. You got it just right!" In *Isaiah*, we are told, "For your Creator is your husband" (54:5). In this instance, I experienced the 'male' nature of God, not in the protection but (and this is said by a female with tongue in cheek) God is always right and He does like to have the last word!

Our God is a God who speaks, because He wants to draw close to us. It is up to us to listen! However, if we try to do this 'under our own steam', we will come a cropper, as *Proverbs* warns, "Do not think of yourself as wise" (3:7), or "Do not be wise in your own opinions" (ISV). We need help, and that help comes in the form of the Holy Spirit. Whatever we do under our own steam, can be not only fruitless, but can also prove to be a stumbling block, in which we begin to lose our way, our direction. As Jesus said, "But the Advocate, the Holy Spirit, whom the Father will send in my name, will teach you everything and remind you of all I have said to you" (*John* 14:26). Jesus echoed Isaiah (54:13) "Your sons will all be taught by Yahweh" when He said, "It is written in the prophets, 'and they shall all be taught by God'" (*John* 6:45). We need to allow the Holy Spirit to not only teach us, but also to guide us. To do that, we need to learn to listen to His voice.

In *Isaiah* 5:1–4, we hear the parable of the vineyard owner. "My friend had a vineyard on a fertile hillside. He dug the soil, cleared it of stones, and planted choice vines in it. In the middle he built a tower, he dug a press there too. He expected it to yield grapes, but sour grapes were all that it gave. And now, inhabitants of Jerusalem and men of Judah, I ask you to judge between my vineyard and me. What could I have done for my vineyard that I have not done? I expected it to yield grapes. Why did it yield sour grapes instead?"

This vineyard metaphor in Isaiah was a parable used to describe God's relationship with His people Israel. The Israelites' identify flowed from the conviction that its people were unique as God's chosen people. After all, He had spoken to them through the Prophets! But they didn't always listen! Isaiah used this parable to make them aware that even if they were specially chosen – choice vines – that didn't mean they could disregard God's Word, or put their own interpretation on it, which would allow them to carry out injustices.

It shows us that we can do all the right things, make correct choices – planted on a hillside – acted correctly when the soil was prepared – chose the best vines – even was so confident of a successful crop, that he made a wine press, and in case someone sabotaged the crop, a watch tower was built. What a disaster that must have been when after all the effort made, only sour grapes were produced, grapes that were useless! And yet we can also be guilty of this, whether it is in our churches, our parishes, our families, when we act without the guidance of the Holy Spirit. Just because we are doing a work for God, we feel He will bless it. We may ask for the guidance, then not listen to the answer but actually tell God what we are going to do to convert hearts to him. We put the cart before the horse, and then we wonder why our efforts are in vain. When the fruit that is yielded is 'sour', we may become bitter inside, and our hearts become hardened. Just like Zachariah, we may still continue 'God's work' but with a hardened heart. Not only do we need to take time to listen to God through the whisperings of the Holy Spirit, we also need to take time to 'listen' to ourselves, our words and to analyse them, under the guidance of the Holy Spirit. For this, in due course, will lead to an understanding of our actions, and in turn will show what is actually in our hearts, *not what we would like to be in our hearts*, but what is actually in them!

I think it is important to note that it is really important to meet as a Christian community not only to pray, worship, share and socialise, but also to listen, reflect and come to understand and help others to understand the words of God. However, the lessons we learn need then to penetrate our hearts so that they can influence our actions, illuminate the darkness within us. We need to remember that like Zachariah, being in a temple or church is not going to bring us closer to God. As one Christian pastor said, "Sitting in a church is no more going to make you into a Christian than sitting in a garage will change you into a car." It just isn't going to happen! However, we are much more likely to hear, listen and respond to the Word of God when we attend a church, and more importantly be more reflective, to look inward, so that our hearts can become softened.

The Holy Spirit is the voice of God. We need to listen to Him to get our lives back on track, to come back into harmony with God. He is the one who will open our mind to understand the scriptures, revealing the hidden meaning. Equipped with the love of God, the friendship of Jesus, and the guidance of the Holy Spirit – knowing that He has called us and chosen us – we can continue our spiritual journey with joy and confidence.

Chapter Six

"Many are called but few are chosen" (Matthew 22:14)

Throughout the Bible, there are examples of men and women being chosen to be leaders, prophets, or even as in the case of Mary, to be the Mother of God. They all came from different backgrounds, and were certainly at different stages of their journey when they were called or chosen for a special ministry. Although some deserved the calling, as their life reflected their dedication to God, such people as Samuel, Joseph, Elijah, Elisha, Abraham, etc. to name but a few, however, there were others who did not always lead exemplary lives, their misdeeds included murder, adultery, and even worshipping other gods. In fact, in the family tree of Jesus, there were some quite unsavoury characters. As king, David had arranged the death of Uriah the Hittite to cover his adultery with Bathsheba. There was Jacob, who with encouragement from his mother Rebekah, tricked his brother Esau out of his birth right. King Solomon, known for his wisdom, the son of David and Bathsheba, in later years, and encouraged by his many wives, shifted his allegiance to other gods. Even the suitability of the Apostles had a big question mark hanging over them. Indeed, if Jesus had sent off to a recruitment agency, with a list of requirements needed for the job of a disciple, not one of the group that are known today as the twelve Apostles would have appeared on that list, not one! They wouldn't even have got through the first hurdle, never mind the interview.

So the big question is why are some chosen and not others? Why did Jesus choose the twelve? What was special about them? Why does it appear God chooses some and not others? After all, according to Saint Paul in his letter to the Romans, "God does not have favourites" (*Romans* 2:11). So if God does not have favourites, therefore it would stand to reason that we should all be treated the same. Jesus gives us a deeper understanding of this dilemma in the parable of 'The Wedding Feast', where everyone got invited to the wedding celebration of a king's son. However, not all took up the invitation, and of those that did turn up, one was not wearing a wedding garment, and consequently was thrown out of the banquet. In this parable, Jesus was making the point that all are invited to become a part of the kingdom of God, to come into a personal relationship with God, but the onus is on us, on how we actually *respond to that call; that invite.* However, God has given us a free will. He won't force us to love Him, or to choose to follow Him. That decision is ours! He just waits patiently, ready to help us when we call, ready to welcome us back into the family, but He will never, ever, force us.

Before we get too comfortable and self-righteous, feeling we have responded whole-heartedly to that call, we need to remember not only Zachariah carrying out his priestly duties in the temple with a hardened heart, but also other examples, throughout the Old and New Testament, of men and women carrying out God's work, but whose hearts were hardened. Indeed, one prime example was Judas, one of the twelve original disciples of Jesus and son of Simon Iscariot. Judas played a notorious role in betraying Jesus. His betrayal has often been debated and he remains a controversial figure today in Christian history, because his betrayal is seen as setting in motion the events that led to Jesus' crucifixion and resurrection which, according to traditional Christian theology, brought salvation to humanity, so his action is seen as being ambiguous, serving a purpose, while carrying out an treacherous act.

However, when discussing Judas, it is very easy to get side tracked, getting involved in issues of free will or the fact that Jesus had predicted the role Judas would play in the crucifixion, and there is a danger of when we start debating our opinions of the issue, we will miss an important part of the betrayal of Jesus by Judas, the fact that he had become a very special friend of Jesus, and while still masquerading as a close confidante, he stabbed Jesus in the back, figuratively speaking. Judas had not only responded to the call to become a disciple but he was especially chosen by Jesus as one of his twelve Apostles. The Gospels of Matthew, Mark, and Luke state that Jesus sent out 'the twelve' (including Judas) with power over unclean spirits and with a ministry of preaching and healing: Judas clearly played an active part in this apostolic ministry alongside the other eleven.

He was also there when Jesus spoke the words in the synagogue at Capernaum, "He who eats my flesh and drinks my blood lives in me and I live in him" (*John* 6:56–57). On hearing these words, many of his followers said, "This is intolerable language" (*John* 6:60), and, "Many of the disciples left and stopped going with him" (*John* 6:66). Then Jesus said to the Twelve, what about you, do you want to go away too? Of course Peter answered on their behalf, "Lord, who shall we go to? You have the message of eternal life" (6:68). Judas then had the perfect option to leave but obviously he didn't, even though Jesus went on to say, "Have I not chosen you, you Twelve? Yet one of you is a devil," a wolf in sheep's clothing! It would appear that Judas was so immersed in his own situation that he didn't 'hear' the words, he certainly didn't identify with them for if he had, he would probably have acted in a different way. Sometimes we are so busy looking at 'the splinter in our brother's eye', we 'never notice the plank in our own' (*Matthew* 7:3–4). We have to be careful that we are not so busy looking outward, at those around us, even so far as judging them that we forget to look inward. Judas needed to look inward. He had been called and had been chosen, for a special ministry, yet even though he had become a special friend of Jesus, he like the other disciples had a sinful nature, but unlike the other Apostles, from interpreting his actions, it would appear that he refused to acknowledge it.

Judas was, "A thief; he was in charge of the common fund and used to help himself to the contributions" (*John* 12:6). However, I do feel that there was more to Judas' betrayal than his greed. We learn from Jewish literature that Judas came from a rich family and so to betray Jesus for thirty pieces of silver, which in the time of Jesus, would have been about four hundred pounds, a small amount, it just doesn't quite add up. When the Twelve set out at the beginning of the ministry, they would have been regarded with awe. However, towards the end of the ministry, things were changing. Jesus was openly challenging those in the Jewish authorities and making known enemies. Jesus and his disciples were not being shown the same respect, almost adoration that had occurred at the beginning of the ministry.

So why did Judas betray not only Jesus but also his friends? When googling the word 'betray', the dictionary gives the meaning to 'expose (one's country, a group, or a person) to danger by treacherously giving information to an enemy'. Therefore by using the word 'betrayal', the act of Judas was viewed as a treacherous deed by all four of the Evangelists, indeed Matthew in Chapter 26 uses the words betrayed/betray five times, which would suggest they, the disciples, also felt let down by a friend. Judas was someone they had trusted, laughed with, shared a huge part of their life with, grew spiritually with, and all the time his heart was becoming hardened. His deeds had also revealed what was in his heart. The saddest thing about betrayal is it never comes from your enemies. As Jewish Sages teach: 'By our actions we bring our thoughts to the awareness and consciousness of others'.

Could pride have played a part in Judas' downfall, or could it have been jealousy, or both? Was Judas' pride hurt when Jesus chose Peter, James and John to accompany him up the mountain, for the very deep spiritual encounter that became known as The Transfiguration, as told in the Gospels of Matthew, Mark, and Luke, but also referred to in John's Gospel. Indeed, if that was not bad enough, when they came down from the mountain, Jesus berates His disciples because they could not cast out an evil spirit, Judas would have been included in that group.

As well as pride, Judas could very well have been jealous of Peter, James and John and their relationship with Jesus. We know that the Disciples argued about who was the greatest. What's the betting that Judas was right there in the middle, having started the argument? There would appear to be jealousy within the group, as some were seen as being favourites. It is generally agreed that John is the one referred to 'as the disciple Jesus loved' (*John* 13:23). In his book *God's Love for Us*, Chaim Bentorah states that in the Greek and Hebrew language, there are different words for love, depending on the context. He argues that the word for 'love' used in this setting was 'Racham' – a reciprocal love. It wasn't that Jesus loved John more but that John was able to return or complete that circle of love; something someone with bitterness in their heart could not do.

This however is only speculation but where there is pride and ambition, there is failure. "Wherever you find jealousy and ambition, you find disharmony, and wicked things being done" (*James* 3:16). Being ambitious can be a very good thing, especially when it is being ambitious in the spreading of the Word, or of in the work of the Lord. However, when coupled with pride or jealousy, it can be a very destructive force. So although we don't know for certain, what motive caused Judas to betray Jesus, even taking into account the manner of Judas' death, we can assume that through his scheming, his act of betrayal, Judas' heart was bitter. "Bitterness is in the heart of the schemer" (*Proverbs* 12:20).

However, it wasn't only the Disciples who had been very deeply hurt by Judas' betrayal; Jesus had too, even more so, because on the night of the Last Supper, Jesus had told the Twelve that He had longed to eat this Passover meal with them before He suffered. Yet later on, "While at supper with his disciples, Jesus was troubled in spirit and declared, 'I tell you most solemnly, one of you will betray me.'" Quite simply, Jesus was deeply hurt too by Judas' actions. He had loved Judas, unconditionally, just as He had loved the others, even though Jesus had known what was in Judas' heart, He had never given up on him.

Judas had listened to all the words of Jesus, had experienced the ministry of Jesus at first hand, had heard the parables, and yet the message, that of God being a loving forgiving God, had not taken root in his heart. "When he found that Jesus had been condemned, Judas his betrayer was filled with remorse and took the thirty silver pieces back to the chief priests and elders, 'I have betrayed innocent blood.' 'What is that to us?' they replied, 'That is your concern.' And flinging down the thirty pieces in the sanctuary, he made off, and went and hanged himself" (*Matthew* 27:3–6). He hadn't understood 'forgiveness', he couldn't accept God's forgiveness because he couldn't forgive himself.

What a contrast between Judas' betrayal of Jesus and that of Peter. "Then they seized him and led him away, bringing him into the high priest's house, and Peter was following at a distance. And when they had kindled a fire in the middle of the courtyard and sat down together, Peter sat down among them. Then a servant girl, seeing him as he sat in the light and looking closely at him, said, 'This man also was with him.' But he denied it, saying, 'Woman, I do not know him.' And a little later, someone else saw him and said, 'You also are one of them.' But Peter said, 'Man, I am not.' And after an interval of about an hour, still another insisted, saying, 'Certainly this man also was with him, for he too is a Galilean.' But Peter said, 'Man, I do not know what you are talking about.' And immediately, while he was still speaking, the rooster crowed. And *the Lord turned* and *looked* at Peter. And Peter remembered the saying of the Lord, how he had said to him, 'Before the rooster crows today, you will deny me three times." When Peter *looked into the face of Jesus,* he realised what he had done, he really regretted his action, his words, "And he went out and wept bitterly" (*Luke* 22:54–62 – ESV). He repented, when the words of Jesus came to him. He wept; he was sorry, but he didn't let it deter him, turn away and give up. He had also listened to the words spoken about forgiveness and those words had penetrated his heart. He was able to forgive himself for his weakness; was able to acknowledge what he had done, not blame those around him for putting him in that situation, his pride. He was able to say the word 'sorry' straight from his heart.

Unlike Judas, Peter was able to forgive. The ability to forgive is one of the resources that God has given to us and it is therefore up to us to use it. In Hebrew, the word for forgiveness is '*mechilah*', which is related to the word '*mochul*', meaning a circle. Life is often portrayed as a circle which encompasses all of our experiences and relationships in what should be one harmonious, seamless whole. However, the circle is broken when someone hurts us. Forgiveness is the way we heal the wound. Forgiveness means oh such more than merely forgiving the person who hurt us, but it also involves forgiving ourselves, forgiving God, even forgiving life itself with all its cruel twists and turns. Forgiveness is letting go and building the confidence necessary to experience healthy and positive growth. It is the key to unlocking the chains that others may have put on us; no longer need we remain locked in the past as a victim of circumstances, perpetuated by negative life-patterns through blame and anger. Forgiveness means letting go of the past, the painful memories. It is good to let everything go from the negative experience but at the same time, we need to retain what was learnt, whether it be about ourselves or others. Indeed, painful situations when confronted can shine a light into our darkness and help us to see what is going on within our hearts. When we examine the situation, it can be quite illuminating as it is often ourselves that we unconsciously refuse to forgive.

In Judas' situation, he couldn't forgive himself. *Proverbs* 16:25 says, "There is a way that seems right to a man, but its end is the way of death." Constantly in our journey through life, we need to make choices. Even children as young as three are being challenged about their actions and asked them to think about the choice they have made. "Was it a good or a bad choice?" Obviously, this is asked when they have made what could be considered as a 'bad' choice, where they have hurt or upset another child. It is a lesson we all need to learn and retain, and that is the choices we make will either take us in a positive, life-giving direction or take away the opportunity to be a loving person. We have to make the choice to forgive ourselves. Actually forgiving ourselves does not let us off the hook, it certainly does not justify what we have done, and it is not, as often supposed, a sign of weakness. Rather, forgiveness is a choice that takes courage and strength, and it gives us the opportunity to overcome our weakness rather than remaining a victim, held within chains of our own making.

When we refuse to forgive ourselves, it can be seen as a form of pride, as we are using a different set of rules, a higher set of standards for our self over others. When we can find it within our self to forgive others, but not ourselves, we are saying that we are less capable of making a poor decision than others, are more intuitive, wiser, and more insightful. Therefore, we consider ourselves better than others. When we refuse to forgive ourselves, what we are doing is setting ourselves above others and that is the sin of pride! As *Proverbs* warns us, "Pride goes before destruction, and a haughty spirit before a fall" (*Proverbs* 16:18).

In order to forgive ourselves, we first have to admit to ourselves the truth, admitting not only our failure, but being truthful to ourselves about our emotions, what lead us to act the way we did in the first place. Often that will mean examining our conscience, our sinful nature, and recognising our sin, our pride. The sin of pride, or vanity, is said by some to the foremost of the Seven Deadly Sins, which include greed, lust, envy, gluttony wrath and sloth. The sin from which all others arise, "*inordinate* self-love is the cause of every sin," according to the theologian Saint Thomas Aquinas. It is the *excessive* belief in one's own abilities. Saint Paul warns again the sin of pride in the First *Corinthians* 4:7, "What do you have that you did not receive? And if you did receive it, why do you boast as though you did not?" We need to acknowledge that everything we have, and everything we have accomplished, we have received from God. It is not wrong to feel good about something accomplished; indeed, it is important for us to feel good, but what we do need to do is recognise, and admit, that it could not have been accomplished without God, we need to give the glory, the praise, back to Him. "Whatever you eat, whatever you drink, whatever you do *at all*, do it for the glory of God" (*1 Corinthians*: 31),

When on earth, Jesus spoke about the sin of pride and even openly condemned the behaviour of the scribes and the Pharisees who were using their position to bring glory to themselves and not to the God they claimed to serve. "Everything they do is done to attract attention, like wearing broader phylacteries and longer tassels, like wanting to take the place of honour at banquets and in the synagogues, being greeted obsequiously in the market squares and having people call them Rabbi" (*Matthew* 23:5–8), Many Pharisees prided themselves in their strict avoidance of obvious, outward sin. In these challenging words, Jesus was rebuking them for their obsession with outward perfection, while not being aware of the presence of inner sin, which didn't fall within the boundaries of their man-made rules. "Oh you Pharisees! You clean the outside of cup and plate, while insides yourselves you are filled with extortion and wickedness" (*Matthew* 23:11), Jesus was challenging their self-righteousness. From their outward actions, they had fallen prey to the human desire for recognition and praise. They were looking for man's approval, not God's, wanting people to think of them as being holier, cleverer, wiser and more important than those around them. Jesus was telling them that they needed to become humble. Jesus warns us of the dangers when our actions are rooted in pride, "Anyone who exalts himself will be humbled, and anyone who humbles himself shall be exalted." In the letter of James, he reinforces Jesus' message, "Humble yourself before the Lord and he will lift you up" (*James* 4:10).

Jesus is our ultimate example of humility. Out of obedience to His Father, He humbled Himself all the way to the point of death on the cross. The Bible says because of this that God exalted Him just like how it says He will exalt us (*1 Peter* 5:6–7). "And being found in human form, He humbled Himself by becoming obedient to the point of death, even death on a cross. Therefore God has highly exalted Him and bestowed on Him the name that is above every name, so that at the name of Jesus every knee should bow, in heaven and on earth and under the earth, and every tongue confess that Jesus Christ is Lord, to the glory of God the Father" (*Philippians* 2:8–11).

In the Gospel of John, Jesus speaks frequently of His relationship with the Father, of the motives by which He is guided, of His consciousness of the power and spirit in which He acts, which can be attributed to the total act of humility. "The Son can do nothing by Himself" (*John* 5:19). He was nothing, that God might be all. Of His own power, His own will, and His own glory, of His whole mission with all His works and His teaching, Jesus said, "I can do nothing by myself; I can only judge as I am told to judge, and my judging is just, because my aim is to do not my own will, but the will of the one who sent me" (*John* 5:30–31). "As for human approval, this means nothing to me" (*John* 5:41). "Because I have come from heaven, not to do my own will but to do the will of the one who sent me" (*John* 6:38). "My teaching is not from myself: it comes from the one who sent me" (*John* 7:16).

Jesus' humility was simply the surrendering of Himself to God, to allow Him to do in Him what He pleased, regardless of whatever men around might say of Him, or do to Him. This is the root and nature of true humility. Jesus teaches us where true humility takes its rise and finds its strength is in the knowledge that it is God who works all in all, that our place is to yield to Him in perfect resignation and dependence, in full consent to be and to do nothing of ourselves. When we feel that this life is too high for us and beyond our reach, it must urge us to seek the help of Jesus, to call out in humility for His help. He himself told us to come to him, "Come to me, all you who labour and are overburdened, and I will give you rest. Shoulder my yoke and learn from me, for I am gentle and humble in heart, and you will find rest for your souls. Yes, my yoke is easy, my burden light" (*Matthew 11*: 28–30). Jesus also humbled Himself before men too, to be the Servant of all. "Yet here am I among you as one who serves" (*Luke* 22:27).

When we don't humble ourselves, we are really saying we don't trust God. When we do humble ourselves, we are trusting God with what's going on in our lives while believing He is the provider instead of ourselves. However, we have to be careful we don't fall into the trap of false humility. Uriah Heep, the fictional character created by Charles Dickens in his novel *David Copperfield*, was notable for his cloying humility, and insincerity, making frequent references to his own 'umbleness'. The oxymoron was proud of his humility, certainly applied in this case.

On several occasions, I have heard of groups who meet and pray together using the phrase, "We listen to each other in humility." Which begs the question, why listen in humility? The only answer can be because some of us are more spiritually advanced but we can still learn from those who less spiritual-minded. No, we learn from each other!

Just as pride can lead to a high self-esteem, a lack of pride, or false humility can lead to a low self-esteem, which in turn can lead to depression and self-destructive behaviour. Of the seven deadly sins, pride is the only one with a virtuous side. It is certainly a good thing to have pride in one's country, in one's community, and especially in one's self. The danger happens when our pride becomes excessive, we hold ourselves, our thought, our intellect, our wisdom, in high esteem. That is when we need to readdress the balance, to turn back from the road that we are on and follow the path of humility.

The act of humbling ourselves or Humility is one of the Seven Virtues, or specific opposites of the Seven Deadly Sins. According to Saint Teresa of Avila, "It is most certain truth, that the richer we see ourselves to be, confessing at the same time our poverty, the greater will be our progress, and the more our humility." There is a general misunderstanding that being humble is a form of weakness when in actual fact it is the opposite, for the one who practises humility is the strong one.

According to Janet Chismar, writing in the Billy Graham Evangelistic Association (*billygraham.org*), there are ways we can show humility, each of them demonstrating a strength, not weakness, but strength of character.

"We need to:

Routinely confess your sin to God *(Luke 18:9–14)*.

Acknowledge your sin to others *(James 3:2, James 5:16)*.

Actively submit to authority…the good and the bad *(1 Peter 2:18)*.

Receive correction and feedback from others graciousl*y (Proverbs 10:17, 12:1)*.

Accept a lowly place *(Proverbs 25:6–7)*.

For all things give thanks to God *(1 Thessalonians 5:18)*.

Let your words be for the improvement of others *(Ephesians 4:29–30)*.

Treat pride as a condition that always necessitates embracing the cross, *(Luke 9:23)*.

Take wrong patiently *(1 Peter 3:8–17)*

Choose to serve others *(Philippians 1:1, 2 Corinthians 4:5, Matthew 23:11)*.

Be quick to forgive *(Matthew 18: 21–35)*."

Forgiveness is regarded as possibly one of the greatest acts of humility we can do. Forgiveness is actually the denial of self, and subsequently when we deny self, we are not insisting on our way and our justice. Throughout the Bible, there are constant references to forgiveness and the message God our Father gives, through His prophets, and through His Son Jesus, is that it is in *our* own best interest to forgive! He is not talking about what is in the best interest of the person who needs to be forgiven. We are the ones who God is trying to protect. We are the ones who receive the most benefit from forgiveness, not the other person. A spirit of unforgiveness complicates and compromises our daily walk with God. It keeps us in chains so we can't be free, it can imprison us, and cause us to go off in a wrong direction. Forgiving others releases us from anger and allows us to receive the healing we need. The whole reason God has given us this specific direction is because it can hinder, or change our journey. God's love for us is beyond our comprehension. Forgiving others *spares us* from the consequences of living out of an unforgiving heart. However, sometimes it is much easier said than done. "Everyone says forgiveness is a lovely idea, until they have something to forgive," C.C. Lewis. Forgiving others may seem to be a choice, and in one sense it is a choice, but Jesus spoke often about the need to forgive. He has given us specific direction in numerous Scriptures, all of which can be summed up in just one word – forgive! God's Word says, "And when you stand praying, if you hold anything against anyone, forgive him, so that your Father in heaven may forgive you your sins" (*Mark* 11:25). "Do not judge, and you will not be judged. Do not condemn, and you will not be condemned. Forgive, and you will be forgiven" (*Luke* 6:37). If we can't truly forgive *from the heart,* we can't truly love.

"God's love shows us how to forgive, His forgiveness shows us how to love," Kathy Carlton Willis states in her poster published on *CBN* website, and in the words of Mother Theresa, "If we really want to love, we must learn how to forgive." When we love, we become vulnerable and consequently can easily be hurt, and it is that hurt that is so difficult to forgive.

By loving Judas, Jesus had given Judas the ability to hurt Him, this love of one of His friends had made Jesus vulnerable. As C.S. Lewis wrote in *The Four Loves*, "To love at all is to be vulnerable. Love anything and your heart will be wrung and possibly broken. If you want to make sure of keeping it intact, you must give it to no one, not even an animal. Wrap it carefully round with hobbies and little luxuries; avoid all entanglements. Lock it up safe in the casket or coffin of your selfishness. But in that casket, safe, dark, motionless, airless, it will change. It will not be broken; it will become unbreakable, impenetrable, and irredeemable. To love is to be vulnerable."

When we love, we also become vulnerable and thus can be deeply hurt and wounded when this love is betrayed especially by someone we have considered a friend, a confidante. It is this betrayal of someone close to us that is the hardest to forgive. It is only when we stop feeling the pain can we then start the process to forgive. And yet only a few days after Jesus experienced the pain caused by the betrayal, He was able to say, with His dying breath, in excruciating pain whilst looking up to His Father, "Father, forgive them; they know not what they do" (*Luke* 23:34). Jesus was looking up, not inward at the hurts or pains he had endured. He was looking upward to His Father. Thus His final act was an act of pure, selfless love, not from a bitter, angry, twisted heart, but from a heart so full of love and forgiveness.

Chapter Seven

"But I put my trust in you, Yahweh,
I say, 'You are my God.'
My days are in your hand, rescue me,
from the hands of my enemies and persecutors;
Let your face smile on your servant,
save me in your love" (Psalm 31:14–17).

When we respond to the call, 'come follow me', the views, opinions and ideas we had at the beginning of our journey will often be challenged. What is important is not the challenge but how we respond to it, for it is this that will define us. Either we use it to amend our thinking and consequently grow, or ignore it, and even in some cases we turn against the person challenging us. Even when we are presented with new evidence, sometimes we don't want to face it, use it or confront it, we would rather bury it, so we don't have to deal with it.

Many years ago, I took part in an archaeological dig in the Negev Desert in Israel, working on a Nabatean settlement. The Nabateans were a nomadic tribe who began migrating gradually from Arabia during the sixth century BC. Over time, they abandoned their nomadic ways and settled in a number of places ranging from Jordan to northern Arabia. At its height in the century or so prior to and after the birth of Christ, the Nabataean empire included parts of Jordan, Israel, Egypt, Syria and Saudi Arabia. The seat of the kingdom was Petra, a city that the Nabataeans had carved by hand from the rose-red cliffs in southern Jordan.

The professor in charge of the dig was a well-respected archaeologist who had written two books on the Nabateans. However, when certain finds were made, he would call out in anguish, "No, no, bury it again." Why? Because the find would have contradicted his previous theory making him rethink and consequently amending his views, but not only that it also meant admitting he had got it wrong. How often do we, when faced with new ideas or evidence, or challenged about our views and opinions, ignore the evidence, bury it, turn our backs or even worse, turn on the person who is challenging us.

In the early church, there is an account of someone being persecuted because he dared challenge the views of respected religious leaders, and that person was Stephen, the first Christian martyr. Seven Deacons were elected leaders by the Early Christian church to minister to the community of believers in Jerusalem and to enable the Apostles to concentrate on 'prayer and the Ministry of the Word' (*Acts* 6:5). Stephen was one of the seven. According to the narrative in *Acts*, they were identified and selected by the community of believers on the basis of their reputation and wisdom, being 'full of the Holy Spirit', and their appointment was confirmed by the Apostles.

Stephen had provoked opposition in the Synagogue of the Freedmen and in return, some people from the Synagogue were persuaded to give false witness against him. "So they procured some men to say, 'We heard him using blasphemous language against Moses and against God'" (*Acts* 6:11). They were prepared to tell lies, to achieve a means, an outcome they wanted, by wilfully distorting the truth. Perhaps that is why to bear false witness is right up there with the Ten Commandments, along with adultery and murder. Just like Jesus, Stephen was also accused of saying something he hadn't. These men were deliberately misleading.

It is bad enough having words spoken reflected and used against you, but how much worse to have honest words, distorted so they can take on a whole new meaning. When

Isaiah foretold the coming of Jesus, he claimed that the Messiah would, "not judge by appearances, he gives no verdict on hearsay" (*Isaiah* 11:3). The definition of hearsay is the information received from other people which cannot be substantiated. It is therefore really important not to listen to hearsay as the keyword in this definition is being 'substantiated', which in many situations is difficult, if not sometimes impossible, to establish the validity of the words spoken.

We need also to remember that when it comes to hearing words that someone was supposed to have said, regardless who they are, even someone who may be high up in authority, or in religious life, it doesn't matter, as it is second hand, it must be regarded as such, and taken with a pinch of salt. Better not to listen to it at all, because it will influence the way we think and speak about a person. People can be very controlling and manipulative and by repeating negative comments, they can influence the way we think about, and speak to others. They can, in a subtle way, control the way we respond to those around us. They can even take away our peace of mind. Instead of listening to them, we need to recognise the situation, for what it is, challenge them, and then speak to the person directly, not in an accusing way but in a gentle way, seeking to find the truth.

When we listen to reported speech, it may be verbatim, but it is like a film director bringing to 'life' a story written by someone else. He will put his interpretation, his understanding into the story. Although the reported speech may contain the full truth, or elements of the truth, it must be remembered it is being used for a purpose, and that intention may be good or bad. Even when it has been collaborated by someone else, that still does not mean it is necessarily true. Words spoken when they are repeated are used creatively. Although the words used are exactly the same spoken, and in the right order, they are being used for a different reason, in a different situation. Therefore, they can take on a completely different meaning. They are being taken out of the context, used and may be reflected with a different expression, tone, or using different body language, which can lend to ambiguity.

How many people are walking around today deeply hurt; unable to forgive, with some even some having had their lives ruined, and all by false accusations, or by so called 'well-meaning' people, telling them negative things others have said about them. Man's inhumanity to man. Saint Paul in his first letter to Timothy, encourages all the believers to be an example, "In the way you *speak* and *behave*" (4:12). Actually, the two are linked, both the way we speak and the way we behave. Our words, like our actions, show what is in our hearts. They need to be used wisely. Words can build up or pull down, can bless or curse, can create or destroy. We need to learn to listen to not only the words spoken but what a person is actually saying.

Once in a 'Philosophy for Children' lesson, a class of eight-year-olds were shown a picture of two boys. One boy was a large teenager, the other was a small child cowering in front of him with tears running down his cheeks. The object of the lesson was to challenge their perception of a bully. Initially questions were given concerning the picture. Then with mutual agreement, one question in particular was chosen to be discussed in depth. In this case, it was, "Is this a picture of someone being bullied?" When answering the question, the children cannot go off on a tangent, they need to listen carefully and follow on from what the previous person has said. Obviously the perception was challenged, with all agreeing on the definition of a bully, someone who makes us do something against our will. The dictionary gives the definition as 'a person who uses strength or influence to harm or intimidate those who are weaker.' At the conclusion of the lesson, there was an agreement that just because the older boy looked bigger and aggressive, he may not actually have been a bully. The small child could actually have been bullying the older boy's brother and he was telling him off, consequently the smaller boy was crying.

There were two factors important in this lesson. Firstly, the children were learning to listen and respect what others were saying, they were open and willing to have their ideas challenged. Secondly, all is not as it appears. Sometimes we too, like the children, need to have our perception of a bully challenged. Bullies can come in all ages, shapes and sizes. They can come from all walks of life, and be in different positions of power. They can even be our 'friends' and abuse the friendship by dictating who we can and can't be friends with, and we play along with their little games, even though we don't feel right or comfortable but because we don't want to upset them, in a way we are a little bit afraid of them. Bullies are normally very ambitious and quite selfish, putting their own needs and wants in front of others, but always they are controlling and manipulative.

A few weeks after the philosophy lesson, I was in the playground when I witnessed a case of bullying. One little girl from a different class was having issues with friends, so went off by herself to play hop scotch. She was totally oblivious to all that was going on around her. Two children, seven-year-olds, from her class came and stood in the middle of the game, intimidating her. She asked them politely to step aside and they ignored her, and persisted with their behaviour, so she pushed them gently out of the way. Immediately they came running to me, accusing the child of hurting them. They had been the ones who had intimidated her, bullied her into doing something she didn't want to do. Not only had I witnessed the incident but many years as a teacher have taught me that the children who come running accusing others of 'not being their friend' or 'of others being unkind to them' are usually the ones who use the threat. "If you don't do what I want you to do, then I am going to tell the teacher/someone higher up in authority." They can be the ones who are bullying. Bullying can be very subtle, and bullies don't always use aggressive behaviour to achieve their ends, words can be used just as effectively as weapons to harm or damage others.

A thought-provoking story appeared on Facebook recently. It told of an elderly man who was jealous of a younger man and spread rumours about him. When the young man heard these lies, he brought the older man to court. The judge asked the accused to write down all he had said, and then on the journey home, he was to tear the paper up into tiny pieces. The pieces of paper were then to be thrown out of the carriage window. (Before I have conservationists yelling at me, I know it is really wrong to disperse with paper in this way, but it really is a good illustration on making a point).

The following morning, both men appeared before the judge. When questioned, the elderly man was able to say with confidence that he had carried out the judge's request and the paper had been duly scattered. On hearing this, the judge demanded, "Now I want you to go and collect up each piece of paper." On hearing this, the accused became despondent, and replied that it was impossible. "Ay, yes," said the judge, "So it is with our words. As soon as they are out of our mouth, we have no control over them. They can become scattered far and wide. So always use them wisely."

When spoken, not only do we not have any control over our words, but they can spread and inflame hatred, or they can stir up all kinds of emotions. Indeed, the reactions to the spoken word can be a reflection of inner prejudices, jealousy or pride. This is what happened in Stephen's situation for although his words were wise, they were used against him because his accusers had closed minds. "They found they could not get the better of him because of his wisdom and because it was the Spirit that prompted what he said" (*Acts* 6:10). They were so caught up in their own pride, their own importance, looking inward instead of upward. C. S Lewis warns us of pride in *Mere Christianity*, "A proud man is always looking down on things and people; and, of course, as long as you are looking down, you cannot see something which is above you."

There is also evidence of anger caused by pride, as the story of Stephen unfolds. When he is brought in front of the

Great Sanhedrin, instead of bowing to their wisdom, he used the opportunity to witness to the fact that Jesus was not only a prophet, but the Messiah, the Chosen One. This was a very brave act as the Great Sanhedrin was made up of a Nasi (President), who functioned as head, and was a member of the court, an *Av Beit Din*, the chief of the court who was second to the Nasi, and sixty-nine general members (Mufla), quite an intimidating, intellectual group, who would have vehemently opposed the idea of Jesus being the Son of God!

However, when confronted by them, Stephen wasn't intimidated and used the opportunity to speak boldly to them, linking the Old Testament with the New, and in so doing, he was showing that the Jewish religion was built upon the foundation of God's calling and promises. He pointed out to them, throughout the history of 'our (Jewish) ancestors' – thus identifying himself as a fellow Jew – how they (both them and their ancestors) had been against the Prophets, as well as the Holy Spirit who spoke through them and the Messiah, whose coming they had predicted. It was when Stephen made this link with them being responsible for the killing of the Messiah, "Now you have become his betrayers, his murders" (*Acts* 7:53), that they turned into an angry mob, "They were infuriated when they heard this and ground their teeth at him" (*Acts* 7:54). Stephen, like many of the Holy men including the prophets, and especially Moses, was suddenly in a very dangerous position. However, this dangerous situation didn't deter them. They refused to be bullied into saying or doing something they did not believe. Through their faith, and with courage, while faced with adversity, they had continued to proclaim the word of God, even when they were faced with a very ugly crowd, ready to tear them to pieces, and God, as in the other dangerous situations, did not abandon them.

A similar story of profound faith causing men to refuse to stand down in the face of adversity, refusing to be intimidated by a powerful person, appears in the Book of Daniel (Old Testament). It is of three men facing death because of their faith, their beliefs, and all brought about through pride and jealousy of their accusers. About 600 BC, King Nebuchadnezzar of Babylon besieged Jerusalem and took captive many of Israel's finest citizens. Among those deported to Babylon were three young men from the tribe of Judah: Shadrach, Meschach and Abednego. During their time in captivity, these three men grew wise and respected as high-appointed officials in Babylon. As is often the case, other Babylonian officials became jealous of them. Through careful plotting and negotiating, these officials were able to get King Nebuchadnezzar to command that all people bow down in worship to a large, (ninety feet high and nine feet wide) golden statue whenever they heard the sound of his musical herald. The punishment for failure to do so was horrific. Anyone who failed to bow and worship the image would be thrown into an immense, blazing furnace.

When Shadrach, Meschach and Abednego refused to bow down and worship the idol and god of Babylon, Nebuchadnezzar addressed them, "Shadrach, Meshach and Abednego, is it true that you do not serve my gods, and that you refuse to worship the golden statue I have erected?" (3:14). "If you refuse to worship it, you must be thrown straight away into the burning fiery furnace, *and where is the god that could save you from my power?*" Words spoken with such pride and arrogance! However, Shadrach, Meshach and Abednego replied to King Nebuchadnezzar in humility and without presumption, "Your question hardly requires an answer: If our God, the one we serve, is able to save us from the burning fiery furnace and from your power, O king, he will save us; and even if he does not, then you must know, O king, that we will not serve your god or worship the statue you have erected" (*Daniel* 3:16–19). In saying this, they demonstrated their knowledge of the power of God and their commitment to his revealed word. The sentiment, so similar to Peter's when Jesus had asked, "What about you, do you want to go away too?" and he replied, "Lord, who should we go to, you have the message of eternal life, and we believe; we know that you are the Holy one of God" (*John* 6:67–68).

There is a story about a man falling off a cliff. On his way down, he manages to grab hold of a sapling growing out of the cliff face. With determination he grabs it, holds on for dear life and calls out, "Is there anyone up there that can help me?" A voice answers, "Yes, Just let go!" A pause, and then the man calls out again, "Is there anyone else up there?" Sometimes when we call for help, we expect the situation to be resolved in a certain way. Shadrach, Meshach and Abednego didn't challenge God's plan for them. Just because they worshipped God, they didn't expect God to do their will, they didn't call on him to have mercy, to save them. Surely if we are doing the Lord's work, we should be rewarded with miracles of His saving power? This is man's thinking, not God's.

Although they were 'bound, fully clothed, cloak, hose and headgear, and thrown into the fiery furnace,' (3:21), they walked into the heart of the flames, praising God, "All you who worship him, bless the God of gods, praise him and give him thanks, for his love is everlasting" (3:89–90). When Nebuchadnezzar approached the mouth of the burning fiery furnace, he shouted, "Shadrach, Meshach and Abednego, servants of the Most High God, come out, come here!" And from the heart of the fire out came Shadrach, Meshach and Abednego, (3:6–27) completely unscathed. Their God, who they had faith in and trusted completely, had saved them. Not only had God saved them, but he had sent down an angel to be with them in their ordeal, "Then he (Nebuchadnezzar) sprang to his feet in amazement, and said to his advisers, 'Did we not have these three men thrown bound into the fire?' They replied, 'Certainly, O king'. 'But,' he went on, 'I can see four men walking about freely in the heart of the fire without coming to any harm. And the fourth looks like a son of the gods.'" (3: 24–26) When he saw the three men alive, joined with a fourth god-like figure, Nebuchadnezzar was forced to reverse his earlier views, his dogmatism. Nebuchadnezzar had had his beliefs, challenged. However when confronted with the evidence, he didn't bury it or ignore it but accepted the power of God. From the way

Nebuchadnezzar behaved after the episode of the fiery furnace, it would appear that he was not a man of genuine faith, he was impressed by the miracles which led him to act in humility and in doing so, he changed his perceptions, however it had not softened his heart. Sometimes, it is just too hard to let go.

Stephen, unlike Nebuchadnezzar, was a man of great faith in the power and love of God. And like Shadrach, Meshach and Abednego didn't waver in his beliefs when faced with adversity. Therefore Stephen, who was "filled with the Holy Spirit, gazed into heaven and saw the glory of God, and Jesus standing at God's right hand" (*Acts* 7:55). Stephen had a vision, and he described this vision to the council. Perhaps he was reminding them of the *Yod*, the need to look up, out of the situation. They had 'ground their teeth', almost like a pack of wolves, ready for the kill. They weren't acting like intelligent men, but of that like a mob, being fed on the aggression of each other, insulted because their intelligence had been called into question, their pride was hurt. In this situation, Stephen was trying to redirect their attention upwards but they didn't want to know. Like children being told something they don't want to hear, they were afraid of his words, "they stopped their ears with their hands; then they all rushed at him, sent him out of the city and stoned him" (*Acts* 7:58). The accusers couldn't wait for a trial so they dragged him out and stoned him; stoning being regarded in Biblical times as a means of cleansing. They had to silence him quickly because he was challenging their beliefs, and if he was right, they were wrong. In their eyes, he was judged, he had to be wrong, and the threat to their religious standing had to be eliminated. He had to be stoned, to be cleansed as he was the one at fault, not them!

When he was being stoned, Stephen does something unusual. In some versions of the New Testament, it is recorded as 'fell to his knees' or in others, 'knelt down'. By using the words 'fell to his knees' or 'knelt down', there is a suggestion that it was a voluntary act. He wasn't brought to his knees by the stoning, but 'fell to his knees' or 'knelt' would suggest he was talking to Jesus the Son of God; he was praying; he was in the presence of God. The last words spoken by Stephen also support this idea, for he said, "Lord, do not hold this sin against them" (*Acts* 7:60). With his dying breath, Stephen, who had previously been so angry with the council, even called them 'betrayers and murderers', suddenly had a complete change of heart. Why? Stephen was not looking up into the heavens (where his help will come from) but up into the face of Jesus. That is why he said, "Lord!" Jesus was there with him. Just as the widow woman of Naim had looked up out of her misery and desperate situation into the face of pure love and compassion, so also was Stephen looking into that same face, but was it also filled with pain? Did Stephen hear the words, "When they hurt you, they hurt me also, for I love you very much?" Was that why, looking into the face of Jesus, Stephen was able to say, the words of forgiveness, from his heart, "Do not hold this sin against them"? At that moment, through his words, it is clear that Stephen didn't want revenge for the harm done to him. What he did want, however, was for those who were stoning him, or those who had falsely accused him, to not only know the truth that Jesus was the Son of God, but more importantly for them, to actually experience the love of Jesus: that love which can't be explained but has so much power, even to change the most hardened of hearts.

Of those standing around the stoning was, 'a young man called Saul' (*Acts* 7:59), someone whose heart was hardened. We are told, "Saul entirely approved of the killing" (*Acts* 8:1), he wasn't involved in the stoning but he agreed with it. Saul, or as he later came to be known as: Paul, had a dramatic conversion, followed by a very, very powerful ministry, which he attributed to the Holy Spirit and his ministry is still ongoing today, though his written words in his letters. He certainly witnessed the love and forgiveness of Stephen, in his death, and many think that was the beginning of his conversion. When we call out for 'help', and are told to "Let go", it may not be the answer we want to hear but we know that when we 'do', we are safely in God's hands, and He only wants the best for us. He loves us with a perfect love, a love we will never fully understand. He just wants us to trust Him, rely on Him and He will do the rest; He will be right there in that situation with us, as was promised in Isaiah:

"Do not be afraid for I have redeemed you;
I have called you by your name, you are mine.
Should you pass through the sea I will be with you;
Or through rivers they will not swallow you up.
Should you walk through fire, you will not be scorched
and the flames will not burn you.
For I am Yahweh, your God,
The Holy One of Israel, your saviour" (Isaiah 43:2–3).

Chapter eight

"I am the vine, you are the branches
Whoever remains in me, with me in him, bears fruit in
plenty" (John 15:5).

At some period of our lives, we pause on our journey, and start questioning its validity, its purpose. Indeed we may even feel we are in a maze, going in the wrong direction, just going around and around without achieving the intended purpose. Indeed we may reach the top, like Stripe on his on his journey on the caterpillar pillar, only to find a void. There was a period in my life where I was in that maze, that caterpillar pillar, where I was searching, was questioning even the validity of existence. After three years of teaching in a Primary School in Essex, I faced the question most of us have faced at one time, 'Surely there must be more to life than this?' My quest took me to Canada. For the next three years, I had the privilege of teaching in one of the most scenic, and officially the wettest town in Canada, the beautiful Prince Rupert, in British Columbia. While there, one of my colleagues, a very level-headed, clever person, invited me along to a weekend Charismatic Retreat. Now, like many similar-minded people, I had heard about these so-called, over the top, arm-waving Christians. From what I had gathered from those who were more informed, this was a new movement where Christians would meet to pray. During the meetings, they would not only speak in a strange language they called 'tongues', but then one person would stand up and speak in tongues, and another member of the Congregation would give an interpretation. I mean really!

Even with this knowledge, when I was invited to the retreat, I actually said, "Yes." Perhaps there was also an element of curiosity involved in my decision, but the main reason for my going was the place where the retreat was being held had a ski hill, but unlike ours, theirs was open. Whatever the reason, that decision took my personal journey in a totally different direction, into a higher and deeper spiritual realm, one on which I have never looked back.

On the Friday evening, I walked into the large auditorium where the Retreat was being held and to my surprise it was completely filled with people, male and female, young, old, and middle-aged. The only expression I can think of to describe my reaction that night was, I was completely hooked, right from that very first moment. It certainly wasn't what I had expected. All the people gathered were singing in a way I had never experienced; they were singing 'gently', meaningfully, to a God they loved – to a personal God – they were singing straight from their heart. As they sang, "Yahweh is the God of my salvation, I trust in him and have no fear," they really meant it, they were singing to God, not at Him. I'd never experienced a religious service so beautiful. On that first night, there was little evidence of the Gifts of the Spirit, but more of the fruits, especially the love, joy and peace.

The following day, an Irish Missionary Priest, OMI, related his experiences in war-torn Biafra. Indeed the Biafran or Nigerian civil war was considered by many to be one of Africa's bloodiest post-independence conflicts. It was fought between the then Eastern Region of Nigeria and the rest of the country, and during the three years it lasted, more than one million people died. News stations throughout the world covered the war, showing tragic, appalling pictures of people, especially children, in various stages of starvation. There was an outcry and funds were raised. However, most people felt helpless, and so to hear of a first-hand account by someone who was not only present but was able to help in a way which almost seemed impossible, was very powerful.

According to the priest, it was indeed a very bleak time. Word came through to him that people in other villages were dying of starvation. In desperation, he sat down and prayed, asking God to help him, to show him what to do, so he could help his people. He opened the Bible at *Matthew* 14:13–21, the miracle of the loaves and fishes. His initial reaction was, "this is not helpful, it was okay for you to do it Lord, you could perform miracles but I can't." So he got up and went out for a walk, all the time thinking of a way to help save the village. While walking, he kept hearing a small voice within him saying, "Go back and read again. What is the first thing that the disciples were ordered to do?" When he did go back and read it, the words almost jumped off the page, as Jesus had ordered the disciples to collect the food and, "bring it to me" (Matthew 14:18). The priest then knew what he had to do. He went out and called the villagers together and explained to them that if they wanted to avoid starvation, they needed to collect all the food they had and to bring it to a central position. Then each day, it would be shared out. The villagers did as asked, and they survived the war, not one died!

On that retreat that weekend, not only did I witness people praying in a new, intimate way with a God they clearly loved, but I also learnt how God could talk to us through the Bible, with the guidance of the Holy Spirit, in what could be described as a dialogue, not a monologue. I wasn't sure if I knew what my understanding of the Holy Spirit was, all I knew was I really wanted Him in my life. When I met the person who had organised the Retreat, Brother Jim, I approached him and said rather naively, but very definitely, "These people have got something I don't have and *I want it*. Just do what you have to do!" Patiently, he explained it would happen when the time was right, and yes it did happen, later that day. "If you then, who are evil, know how to give your children what is good, how much more will the heavenly Father give the Holy Spirit to those who ask him?"

Unfortunately, the Holy Spirit, like God the Father, often gets a poor press. The Holy Spirit (or Holy Ghost, from Old English *gast*, 'spirit') is the third member of The Trinity: the Father, the Son and the Holy Spirit, and is depicted as either a winged dove or tongues of fire, both depictions coming from accounts in the Gospel narratives. The first account comes at the beginning of the public Ministry of Jesus, His Baptism. "Now when all the people had been baptised, and while Jesus after his own Baptism was at prayer, heavens opened and the Holy Spirit descended on him in bodily shape like a dove" (*Luke* 3:21–23). Matthew also gives a similar account, "As soon as Jesus was baptised, he came up from the water, and suddenly the heavens opened and he saw the Spirit of God descending like a dove and coming down on him. And a voice spoke from heaven, 'This is my Son, the beloved; my favour rests on him'" (*Matthew* 3:16–17). John the Baptist also proclaimed, "I saw the Spirit coming down on him from heaven like a dove and resting on him like a dove" (*John* 1:32), and later added, "Yes, I have seen and I am witness that he is the chosen one of God" (*John* 1:34). The Holy Spirit that came upon Jesus to equip Him for His ministry. "The Spirit of the Lord has been given to me, for Yahweh has anointed me. He has sent me to bring good news to the poor" (*Isaiah* 61:1). "The Spirit of the Lord will rest on Him, the spirit of wisdom and understanding, the spirit of counsel and strength, the spirit of knowledge and the fear of the LORD" (*Isaiah* 11:2). "Behold, My Servant, whom I uphold: My chosen one in whom My soul delights. I have put My Spirit upon Him; He will bring forth justice to the nations" (42:1).

Not only did Isaiah's prophecy foretold the coming of Jesus, but it also prophesied that the future ministry of Jesus would be empowered by the Holy Spirit. John the Baptist had also prophesied the coming of Jesus, with power. "I baptise you in water for repentance, but the one who follows me is more powerful than I am, and I am not fit to carry his sandals; he will baptise you with the Holy Spirit and fire" (*Matthew* 3: 1–12). In *John*, Jesus refers to the Holy Spirit as being his connection with the Father, while He was making known the (Good) News, or making known the love the Father has for us. "He who sent me is with me," (8:29). How could the Father be with Him, if it was not through God's Spirit? That *vav*, that connection between heaven and earth. It was this same Spirit that after the Resurrection and before Jesus ascended to His Father, he gave to his disciples. When Jesus was sending out the disciples, to go and make disciples of all nations, he "breathed on them (the disciples) and said, 'receive the Holy Spirit.'"

Although it would appear that the disciples had received the Holy Spirit, they were told to wait until after Jesus had ascended to His Father; it was as though Jesus had planted a seed in their hearts. It wasn't until after the Ascension that the disciples received the outpouring of the Holy Spirit, or that seed flourished and grew. It was while they had gathered together in an upper room to celebrate the Jewish harvest festival of Shavuot, a feast which eventually received the name Pentecost, from the Greek word *Pentekoste*, meaning 'fiftieth day', as it occurred fifty days after the feast of the Passover, when the Holy Spirit descended on them. "And something appeared to them that seemed like tongues of fire; these separated and came to rest on the head of each of them. They were all filled with the Holy Spirit, and began to speak foreign languages as the Spirit give them the gift of speech" (*Acts* 2:3–5).

To me, receiving the Baptism of the Holy Spirit was like the stage in a relationship which could be described as the make or break, the give up or go deeper, the time to make that decision that you want to make a true commitment. It encapsulated both the quiet time before the Ascension when Jesus breathed on the disciples and the more dramatic outpouring of the Holy Spirit, when I felt the love of God very strongly. The Holy Spirt was and has continued to be a great and very highly valued presence in my life, leading and guiding me into higher and deeper spiritual experiences, into a knowledge of the depth of love my Lord has for me. Without Him, I can do nothing. So the question remains, why does the Holy Spirit get such a bad press? Why has the Holy Spirit become the elephant in the Christian room? Could one of the reasons be that the gifts of the Holy Spirit are misunderstood, especially the gift of tongues?

Paul, when writing to the *Corinthians* stated, "There are many different gifts and they are all made available for the common good, from the same Spirit, Lord and God, but of all the gifts" (*1 Corinthians* 12:4). Paul in the same letter identifies nine gifts: the word of wisdom, the word of knowledge, faith, gifts of healing, workings of miracles, prophecy, discerning of spirits, speaking in tongues and interpretation of tongues. With the exception of speaking in tongues, all the gifts are given to aid others in their spiritual journey while, "Tongues is to strengthen the one who uses them, the one with tongues talks for his own benefit" (*1 Corinthians* 14:4). Indeed Paul doesn't see speaking in tongues as part of the highest and most important gifts, he places them at the bottom of his list. However, he does accept that speaking in tongues is a form of prayer, of praise and thanksgiving, and as a way to pray when the mind is perplexed, when we don't know what words to use. "The Spirit too comes to help us in our weakness. For when we cannot choose words in order to pray properly, the Spirit himself expresses our plea in a way that can never be put into words, and God who knows everything in our hearts knows perfectly well what he means, and that the pleas of the saints expressed by the Spirit are according to the mind of God" (*Romans* 8:26–28). Thus the gift of tongues can be used very effectively when praying for the healing of another, when we don't know what words to use, or how to pray. Not only can they be used effectively to help others, but will also aid the person speaking in tongues to come into a closer, more intimate relationship with the Father through His Son. However, it must be stressed that the person with the gift of tongues choses when and if to use them, and then either in silent prayer or in worship where speaking in tongues is a part of the service.

Even today in our churches while some see the Gifts of the Spirit as being incomprehensible, there are those who desire the Gifts for their own selfish reasons, although they may not even be aware of it. In secular Corinth, the elite paraded their gifts and abilities, believing that it was these that gave them status and significance. Indeed this is why Paul had written to them; they were competing with one another for position and power. According to Paul, they (the Corinthians) were status seekers who judged themselves and others on the basis of their spiritual gifts. Consequently in his letter, Paul was very clear about the purpose of the gifts, explaining that there are different gifts, given in different ways, to different people but for the same purpose, *all to build up the body of the Church,* the body of Christ; gifts given to be treasured and cherished but given to be used for the service of others. "There is a variety of gifts but always the same Spirit; there are all sorts of service to be done, but always to the same Lord: working in all sorts of ways in different people, it is the same God who is working in all sorts of different ways in different people, it is the same God who is working in all of them. The particular way in which the Spirit is given to each person is for a good purpose. One may have the gift of preaching with wisdom given him by the Spirit; another may have the gift of preaching instruction given him by the Spirit; and another the gift of faith given by the same Spirit; another again the gift of healing through this one Spirit; one the power of miracles; another, prophecy; another the gift of recognising Spirits; another the gift of tongues, and another the ability to interpret them. All these are the work of one and the same Spirit, who distributes different gifts to different people just as he chooses" (*1 Corinthians* 12:4–11). Indeed it gives God pleasure when we take pleasure in using the gifts He has given to us, when we use them in a selfless way, in the purpose they were intended for, to help us and to help others on their spiritual journey. Even when we use them to bring glory to ourselves and not to others, "God never takes back his gifts or revokes his choice" (*Romans* 11:29).

The Ministry Tool Resource Centre gives a similar definition: a 'Spiritual Gift is a special divine empowerment bestowed on each believer by the Holy Spirit *to accomplish a given ministry* God's way, according to His grace and discernment to be used within the context of the Body of Christ'. Peter in his First Letter states very clearly the need for all who exercise their spiritual gifts to do so only by divine enablement and not in the power of the flesh, not under our own steam. If we are to produce the spiritual fruits, we need to be living in the Spirit, using words of knowledge given directly to us by the Spirit or being used as a channel of Christ's healing love for those around us who are sick or in need; we need to be living in love. As Paul pointed out, "But if there are gifts of prophecy, the time will come when they must fail; or the gift of languages, it will not continue for ever; and knowledge – for this too, the time will come when it must fail" (13; 8–9). "In short, there are three things that will last: faith, hope and love; and the greatest of these is love" (13:13). All we do should be done in love and humility, working to further God's kingdom here on earth, using the tools He has given us, to bring Him, not us, but Him the glory, respect and honour He deserves.

In the First Letter to the Corinthians, Paul also warned about the dangers of the spiritual pride being a basis for some divisions in the church. "Brothers, I myself was unable to speak to you as people of the Spirit; I treated you as sensual men, still infants in Christ. What I fed you with was milk, not solid food, for you were not ready for it; and indeed you are still not ready for it since you are still unspiritual. Isn't that obvious from all the jealousy and wrangling there is among you, from the way you go on behaving like ordinary people? What could be more unspiritual than your slogans, 'I am with Paul' and 'I am with Apollos'?" (*1 Corinthians* 3:1–5). Although the Corinthian church was highly gifted, "The witness to Christ has indeed been strong among you so that you will not be without any of the gifts of the Spirit while you are waiting for our lord Jesus Christ to be revealed" (*1 Corinthians* 16–

7), but according to Paul they, the Corinthians, were far from spiritual; they were still living with worldly views and values. He saw their pride as a form of divisiveness.

It is the same Spirit today that is breaking down the barriers, our divisiveness, with other churches, caused by our pride and our prejudices. The outpouring of the Holy Spirit, according to Paul, is not only to build up our own religious communities but unite us. At the beginning of the twentieth century, there was a definite division between Christians, the Protestants and the Roman Catholics. Indeed Roman Catholics did not enter or worship in protestant churches, as they would have been regarded as a heretic. All that was set to change in the latter part of the century when there was an outpouring of the Holy Spirit, a revival in all churches. In 1960 in Van Nuys, California, the modern charismatic movement began in an Episcopalian Church. After that, the movement spread like wildfire in the Episcopalian and Anglican Church and then among Lutherans, Presbyterians, Methodists and other main-line denominations as well. Between 1962 and 1965, the Roman Catholic Church held the Second Vatican Council, instigated and lead by Pope John XX111. The Council was instrumental for renewal in the self-understanding of the Church, its inner life and its relationship to other Christian traditions, other religions and the world. Those participating in or who lived through the time of the Council felt a profound, exhilarating sense of renewal and virtually experienced a new Pentecost. By 1974, the Notre Dame conference, which involved Catholic Charismatics, was attended by 30,000 people. The movement simply grew and grew.

The Maltese have a saying, "Where God builds a church, the devil builds a chapel," and there is certainly an element of truth in this saying where Renewal is concerned. Just as Christians were coming together to worship in prayer and praising, the Pentecostals, Roman Catholics, Anglian, Methodists, Baptists, Lutherans, Episcopalians, to name but a few, a great opposition was experienced. Fear, suspicion and prejudice, the preconceived and unfounded opinions, began to spread. Although we see how the Spirit worked in the early church, how He guided and empowered believers, but rather than be excited by such activity, we became frightened. If we are truly honest with ourselves, there are times when we find it more comfortable to keep God at arm's length, to focus on our behaviour rather than our hearts, to focus on Him doctrinally rather than experientially, because we're afraid He will call us to step out of our comfort zone, to revaluate our beliefs, our views. We would prefer to believe the fault that causes division lies with others, is because of their pride, their jealousy, but certainly not ours! We just need to step out of our comfort zone, acknowledge our failings and pray with our brothers and sisters, from all different denominations, in the Spirit. David in *Psalm* 133, emphases the importance of unity but how abundantly God will reward us when we live in brotherly love.

> *"How good, how delightful it is for all to live together like brothers:*
> *fine as oil on the head, running down the beard,*
> *running down Aaron's beard*
> *to the collar of his robes;*
> *Copious as a Hermon dew falling on heights of Zion*
> *where Yahweh confers his blessing, everlasting life."*

Jesus also spoke about the importance of unity within all His followers, "I pray not only for these, but for those also who through their words will believe in me. May they all be one. Father, may they be one in us, as you are in me and I am in you" (*John 17*: 20–21) If we pause to reflect on the church's record of disunity, we can easily see how far we have fallen short of Jesus' requirement. If we are resisting the Holy Spirit in our lives, could it be that we are prejudiced, proud of our own beliefs; that our hearts are hardened? While professing to be loving Christians, deep down, is there an area in our hearts which we refuse to surrender to the light? We need the Holy Spirt to help unite us, to allow all denominations to stand side by side, praising, thanking, worshipping God our Father and His son Jesus.

Just as there are divisions between Christian denominations, there can also be division within our churches, congregations, and unfortunately this can be attributed to the outpouring of the Holy Spirit. For those who have received the Baptism, there needs to be an awareness, a sensitivity. Receiving the Baptism of the Holy Spirit is the beginning, not the end, so I find it rather puzzling that new Christians, those who have received the Holy Spirit, will often stand up in public meetings, or more traditional church services, and talk about how their life has changed in a matter of weeks, or even a few months. In some testimonies, they proclaim they were once Jezebels but now they have seen the light. When they are speaking to people who have had little knowledge of the Holy Spirit, they can, quite unintentionally, come across as a little arrogant because of what they are saying. It could be misconstrued as, 'out of all the people gathered, God has especially chosen me to reveal His love.' I am not saying it is wrong to share, in fact it is the opposite, it's really important *to share*, about the coming and workings of the Holy Spirit, but it must be done with people who are on the same stage of the journey as ourselves, as it helps not only the speaker to be able to talk about their experience but it can be very effective in nourishing and inspiring the listeners. We have to be aware that our gifts and the receiving of them is meant to build up the community, and not cause divisions.

Talking about the effect of the Baptism of the Holy Spirit, or a person who has recently been baptized in the Spirit and is giving spiritual advice, can be compared to a young couple at the beginning of a marriage, possibly after only a few months being asked the recipe of a healthy marriage. Not only is it too soon to give advice but it also can be off-putting, especially as they don't really have any answers, and they could be being set up to fail, as a few more months down the line, the marriage could break up. The blind leading the blind. Celebrities have the right idea.

When they are embarking on a new, and very important relationship, which they really want to work, they will hint about it, but won't divulge names or give any details. Why? They have learnt the hard way and that is in order for a relationship to grow and flourish, it needs not only time but also privacy, it needs to develop out of the limelight. We need to witness to the Holy Spirit and the best way to do so initially is through our behaviour, not words, and in time, after years, not months, the testimony of life before and after receiving the Baptism of the Holy Spirit could prove to be very powerful. How much more power can we witness when there is evidence of the fruits of the Spirit in our lives, the love, joy, peace, patience, kindness, goodness, faithfulness, gentleness and self-control.

Another important factor for division within our churches is the way in which Christians baptized in the Spirit worship. People who have received the Holy Spirit may appear more joyful, especially in worship. However, this is in line with Jesus' teaching. The Evangelicals, the Charismatics, are often referred to as the 'happy-clappy, arm waving' Christians. The joy of the Lord may be inexplicable to the one who does not possess it. But, for the believer in Christ, the joy of the Lord comes as naturally as grapes on a vine. Jesus exemplified joy in His ministry to the extent that His enemies actually accused Him of being too joyful! Both *Luke* and *John* refer to the joy Jesus expressed. "It was then that, filled with joy by the Holy Spirit, he said, 'I bless you Father, Lord of heaven and of earth, for hiding these things from the learned and the clever and revealing them to mere children'" (*Luke* 10:21); and in John's gospel, we are told, "I have told you this so that my own joy may be in you and your joy be complete" (*John* 15:11). Jesus promised to share this joy with His followers, "Ask and you will receive, and so your joy will be complete" (*John* 16:24).

Indeed joy is reflected in many of Jesus' parables, including the three stories in *Luke 15*, which mention "rejoicing in the presence of the angels" (*Luke 15*:10). There is the shepherd who is full of joy when he is reunited with his lost sheep; a joyful woman, who went searching for a lost drachma; and a joyful father when his prodigal son had returned. Even in the Old Testament, there is evidence of joy. In the Second Book of Samuel, there is reference to King David, the named author of seventy-six of the Psalms, "When the bearers of the ark of Yahweh had gone six paces, he sacrificed an ox and a fat sheep. And David danced whirling before Yahweh with all his might, wearing a linen loincloth round him" (*2 Samuel*: 13–15). Even Paul spoke of the importance of joy. "For the kingdom of God is not a matter of eating and drinking, but of righteousness and peace and joy in th*e Holy Spirit.*" (*Romans* 14:17) We are meant to be joyful people, joy-filled Christians.

Not only do Spirit filled Christians worship in joy, they also raise their arms while singing. Actually, the custom of raised hands isn't a new phenomenon associated only with the 'charismatics'. It can be traced back to the early years of Israel. Aaron, the first High Priest, raised his hands in prayer as he blessed the Israelites when the sanctuary was first established. The book of Psalms speaks of raised hands regularly: "Because your steadfast love is better than life, my lips will praise you. So I will bless you as long as I live; I will lift up my hands and call on your name" (*Psalms* 63:3–4). Further, the congregation is exhorted to lift their hands in worship of God: "Come, bless the Lord, all you servants of the Lord … lift up your hands to the holy place, and bless the Lord" (*Psalms* 134:1–2). "I stretch out my hands to you; my soul thirsts for you like a parched land" (*Psalms* 143:6). Thus, raised hands in worship may suggest a reaching out for God's presence, blessing, comfort or strength. In *Psalm 63*, the psalmist says he raises his hands to bless God. This symbolizes both gratefulness and joy for the blessings God has given. Indeed, many of the psalms indicate that hands are raised in song and prayer to show thankfulness and joy for God's great works especially in Psalms 134 and 141.

The custom of raising hands during worship was a common practice in the early church, especially during prayer. In Paul's letter to Timothy, he writes, "I desire, then that in every place, the people should pray, lifting up holy hands without anger or argument" (*1 Timothy*: 2–8). In worship when arms are raised, it is the Christian praying, praising God, like David, with their whole body, reaching up to receive blessings, and surrendering to the will and love of God Our father, through His son Jesus, in the Holy Spirit. The practice has become less common in more mainline churches, and in traditional churches; indeed it can be a cause of division. Like the praying of tongues in worship, arms raised should always be done with sensitivity and awareness of the type of service. However on the other hand, arms raised in prayer when praying with other Christians, especially in ecumenical services can be a very powerful and unifying force. In worship, as in all other aspects of life, we should not be judgemental but should be open to the promptings of the Holy Spirit.

We know the Holy Spirit will be given to those who ask as Jesus promised us, "I will send my Spirit to you and he will lead you into complete truth" (*John* 16:13). Jesus also promised, "If anyone loves me, he will keep my word, and my Father will love him, and we shall come to him and make our home with him." That promise is made to every one of us, no matter what church we belong to nor what age we are. However, we must be clear with our motives for wanting the Holy Spirit in our lives. If the Holy Spirit is being sold as the only way to get to heaven, or that we need the Holy Spirit in our lives so we will 'be saved', then are we any better than the 'insurance Catholics' when we asked to receive the Baptism of the Holy Spirit? Do we just see the Holy Spirit as a means to an end?

Quite simply, at the end of the day, all said and done, we need the Holy Spirit; if we but allow Him, He can transform our lives. Not only will The Holy Spirit, when he comes into our lives, lead us in truth but He will also be a unifying presence in our lives, healing the wounds of pain caused by division (*John* 14:23). We need to allow the Holy Spirit into our lives, to challenge us over our ideas of God, our shortcomings, our sinfulness and then perhaps the Holy Spirit will stop being the elephant in the Christian room. In our spiritual life, we must be forever growing, seeing things in new and deeper ways. We need to walk in the way of the Spirit, and follow His direction to the truth, and in turn, He will lead us to the ultimate destination, right into the heart of God.

Chapter 9

"He covers you with his feathers,
And you will find shelter under his wing" (Psalm 91:4).

"I rescue all who cling to me,
I protect everyone who knows my name,
I answer everyone who invokes me,
I am with them when they are in trouble;
I bring them safety and honour,
I give them life long and full" (Psalm 91:14–16).

God is with us every step of the way on our journey and we need to trust in Him and believe in His promises, as in *Psalm 91*. We need to keep looking to Him for direction. We are unique and consequently our journey is unique, no two are the same. So like the journey of the Israelites, we can learn from others' experiences, but it is important not to try and copy them, that is why we need to keep seeking direction, so we may not wander aimlessly in the wilderness. Once a well-known Christian Speaker at our prayer group claimed that her prayer-life was transformed by changing one aspect of her routine. Eagerly, three of us sitting together at the back of the church leant forward to hear what that aspect could be, but on hearing the words, "I set my alarm clock for one hour earlier," promptly sat back. While wanting to ask, "Wasn't there anything else you did?" I felt like the rich young man when Jesus told him that if he wanted to possess eternal life, he needed to give up all his possessions (*Matthew 19*:16–22). We have all different lifestyles, personality, character traits, so what may work for one, may not work for another. On our journey, we shouldn't be trying to take shortcuts or piggy-back on the backs of others. We need to seek guidance on our personal route, our personal direction.

Not only do we need to keep looking up for direction on our unique journey, but there is another important factor to consider and that is time. There is a Jewish saying, 'Do not be hasty in your spiritual journey'. Jesus often spoke on a similar theme, especially in the parables: "The kingdom of heaven is like a mustard seed, which a man took and sowed in his field. It is the smallest of all seeds, but when it has grown, it is the biggest shrub of all garden plants and becomes a tree, so that the birds come and shelter in its branches" (*Matthew* 13:31–32). A mustard seed is minuscule, so from a very small beginning, it can grow into a large powerful tree. However to do so, it needs time and proper nourishment in which to grow and flourish before it can then offer fruit, support, shelter, shade, etc. It needs *time* to mature! If we are too hasty in our spiritual journey, not only may we not grow to maturity, but we may not be exposed to the light, the water and the nourishment needed to grow strong and sturdy, so we can stand firm. By being too hasty, not only will we trip and fall but we could cause others to fall as well; we can be a blockage or a hindrance in their spiritual journey.

In Luke's gospel, we also have the same parable, followed by, "Another thing he said, 'What shall I compare the kingdom of God with? It is like the yeast a woman took and mixed in with *three* good measures of flour till it was leavened all through'" (*Luke* 13:20–22). Not only do both these parables contain a promise that God's work would come to a glorious fulfilment, no matter how small the beginnings, small seed grows to tree-like proportions and a small amount of yeast can cause the dough to expand to a large amount, there is also a deeper meaning. By using the number three, 'mixed in with three good measures,' it could be argued that Jesus was referring to the third letter of the Hebrew Alphabet, the Gimmel, which resembles a bridge, uniting two areas, and in Christian thinking, Jesus is that bridge between us and God the Father. The meaning of the word 'Gimmel' is to nourish until completely ripe, to recompense, to reward. It also represents loving kindness, to be aware of and receive the loving kindness of God, and to be ready to run and show loving kindness to others. The Gimmel teaches us that two opposing forces must be blended together to form a third more complete and perfect entity, but it needs endurance. Primarily, the meaning of the word Gimmel can be summed up in three words, loving-kindness, endurance and nourishment. We need to not only be aware of and rely on God's mercy, His loving kindness, but we need to treat others with the same loving kindness. This in turn will nourish us and give us endurance for our spiritual journey,

Although the parable of the 'wise man who built upon a rock' is primarily about listening and putting into action the Word of God, it could also be argued that that to build a house properly, it has to be dug down deep, which takes time and endurance. The foolish man didn't bother to take the time to dig deep and build firm foundations. He just wanted to get the job done quickly, and of course, "As soon as the river bore down on it, it collapsed; and what a ruin that house became!" (*Luke* 6:49).

Developing a relationship with God is similar to developing any other relationship, it needs time and endurance, to grow and develop; it needs to be set on a firm foundation. In addition to this, it also needs commitment. We can be introduced to someone, and we may feel an immediate connection with them. Initially we will mean to get to know the person more, but life kicks in and suddenly it is not our main priority. We get side-tracked, caught up in the hustle and bustle of everyday life. Consequently, every time we meet the person we keep saying, "We must have that coffee, that lunch" etc., but it never happens until suddenly we are in a position where we really could do with their friendship, their expertise, or just for them to offer an ear to listen to our woes. But because we haven't developed a 'friendship' with them, we are reluctant to get in touch and even if we do, we don't really know how to approach them or what to say. So it can be in our relationship with God the Father, the Son and the Holy Spirit. We are just too busy, too caught up in our materialistic world that it is not until we reach a crisis, a wilderness, an emptiness, that we start to search. It is then we need to believe the promises of Jesus, "Ask and it shall be given to you; search and you will find; knock and the door will be opened to you for the one who asks always receives; *the one who searches always finds;* the one who knocks will *always have the door opened to him*" (*Matthew* 7:7–9).

Sometimes we don't even have to search but just be attentive. In Hosea, we learn, "*That is why I am going to lure her and bring her into the wilderness and speak to her heart" (Hosea 2:14*) or according to New International Version, "Therefore, I am now going to allure her." This is a God who wants to powerfully attract, charm, or tempt us, to draw us to him. There is a beautiful imagery here in the word allure. To me, it conjures up an image of the display, a bird of paradise will put on as part of a mating ritual. It is a very elaborate, bright, colourful dance used to gain the attention of a mate, to lure her to him. It is a very positive word springing from a deep desire, and in the verse from Isaiah, it tells of a God who wants to draw us to Him, so we can share His love. However, as in Moses and the burning bush, we need to be attentive, we need to look up to the heavens, to God. If we are attentive, then we can be prepared for whatever happens on our journey. Consequently, when trials come, they can be used as a signpost to help direct us to go forward, instead of turning back, turning away, or turning inward from the love of God.

Indeed if we are not being attentive or on the alert, when trials come, we immediately look inward, not upward and start questioning God's love for us, "Why is God letting this happen to care for me?" "Why is God punishing me?" The God we have been meaning to get in touch with but never had the time to; The God, who when He tries to talk to us, we don't hear as we are just too busy to listen to Him; The God we have known since a child, and still have those childish ill-formed ideas about. Even the God that we may have spent hours talking to, telling him all our troubles, but because it has been a monologue and not a dialogue, we haven't got to know. Indeed it may just be us, we have been so busy looking inward, we have forgotten top look upwards. We have got the balance wrong!

"*I* am going to bring her, or cause her to come, into the wilderness" (*Hosea* 2: 14). When we are in that wilderness, we need to look up, not inward because that is the time God wants to reach out us, to speak to us tenderly, to speak to us heart to heart. Throughout the wilderness wanderings of the Israelites, God was constantly teaching them things about Himself and about their own sinfulness. He brought them into the wilderness, to the same mountain where He revealed Himself to Moses, so that He could instruct them in what He required of them. He wants to do the same with us. As in the story of the Prodigal Son, Our God, Abba, God the Father, just wants us to come to Him, where we are, as we are. However, how much more does He want us to come to Him where ever we are in a dark place whether it is in our struggles, lost, in the wilderness, stumbling around in the darkness! Whatever our trials, God can use that as the beginning of a new and fruitful relationship. All said and done, He just wants us to come back to Him, no matter what the circumstance. He wants us to come back to Him so He can, and will, transform all our darkness, our trials, perhaps not in the way we want, but in a much better way. In a way that teaches us to love and trust Him.

That is why He sent His only Son Jesus to tell us just how much He loves and cares for us. Jesus demonstrated this love when he gave up His life on the cross. Jesus the link, the bridge between us and God our Father. Jesus, the Light to guide our footsteps in the darkness, so we don't need to stumble around trying to find our way to God Our Father.

Jesus, who promised us that when He went back to His father, He would not abandon us: "I shall ask the Father, and he will give you another Advocate to be with you forever, that Spirit of truth" (*John* 14:17). "But when the Spirit of truth comes, he will lead you into complete truth" (*John* 16:13). The Holy Spirit, joining us with the Father and the Son, the link between the natural and the supernatural. "It is the Spirit that gives life, the flesh has nothing to offer. The words I have spoken to you are spirit and they are life" (*John* 6:63). God shares His thinking with us, if we are prepared to listen, through His Holy Spirit, speaking to us, heart to heart. Quite simply, we need the Holy Spirit in our lives, to help us communicate, to understand, and to grow, mature, and develop into instruments of love, for both God and others.

If we truly want to get to know the God of love, through His Son Jesus, and to be guided by His Holy Spirit, then we need to spend time meditating on His word in the Bible. All the answers to our existence, the purpose of our lives, and how we can live in peace, harmony and love, both with ourselves and with our fellow men, are all there in the Bible, if we but seek them out, with the guidance of the Holy Spirit. As the Psalmist said in *Psalm 119:105*, "Your word is a lamp for my steps, and a light for my path." The Psalmist believed that however it came and in whatever form it existed, the word of God was central to the life of God's people. That sentiment is still so relevant, so true in our world today. It is through the Bible, or the word of God, we can come to know God the Father, God the Son and God the Holy Spirit, and consequently to grow in His love.

Paul in his letters demonstrated so well his understanding of the love Of God and the quest to find that love, which is at the very root of our existence. He claimed that once found, nothing could separate us from this love that God has for us, "For I am certain of this; neither death nor life, no angel, no prince, nothing that exists, nothing still to come, not any power, or height, or depth, nor any created thing can ever come between us and the love of God made visible in Christ Jesus the Lord" (*Romans* 8:38–39).

We can't see the face of God the Father, but we can look up, as did the widow at Naim, into the face of Jesus who is the visible love of God; so filled with love and compassion; just waiting, ready to pour out His Spirit into our hearts. While looking upward, with confidence and knowledge, we can continue our journey, our pilgrimage, into the Heart of the God. The God of Love, in the footsteps of those who have gone before us, while in our hearts singing the oh-so-appropriate hymn: 'The Pilgrims' Progress', the only hymn John Bunyan is credited with writing (which first appeared in Part 2 of *The Pilgrim's Progress*, written in 1684).

He who would valiant (courageous) be 'gainst all disaster,
Let him in constancy follow the Master
There's no discouragement shall make him once relent
His first avowed intent to be a pilgrim.

And then with confidence we can say,

Since, Lord, Thou dost defend us with Thy Spirit,
We know we at the end, shall life inherit.
Then fancies flee away! I'll fear not what men say,
I'll labour night and day to be a pilgrim.

Unlike the pilgrim, we really don't need to labour night and day on our journey, we just need to accept His words and believe in His love, and He will do the rest, as stated in the Hymn 'On Eagles Wings' by Michael Joncas:

And He will raise you up on eagle's wings, Bear you on the
breath of dawn, Make you to shine like the sun, And hold
you in the palm of His hand.